Comparative Political Theory without Borders:

A Journey across Ideological Times and Spaces

Jung In Kang

SOGANG UNIVERSITY PRESS

Comparative Political Theory without Borders: A Journey across Ideological Times and Spaces

Publisher Jong-gu Park
Director Jong Ho Chun

Author Jung In Kang

Published in Sogang University Press
35 Baekbeom-ro, Mapo-gu, Seoul 04107, Korea
Tel +82-2-705-8212 Fax +82-2-705-8612

ISBN 978-89-7273-330-0 93340
₩13,000

Comparative Political Theory without Borders: A Journey across Ideological Times and Spaces

Jung In Kang

Contents

Author's Note

In the main text and footnotes of this book, all Korean, Chinese, and Japanese names appear in the text with the family name preceding the given name (the references follow the English-language practice of given name first). Also, the conventional transliterations for Korean, Chinese, and Japanese are used.

Preface/Acknowledgments

Looking back over my life, I see that *Western-centrism* or what is commonly called *Eurocentrism* has permeated deeply into and shaped my private and public existence, or even my soul, just like racism, patriarchy, classism, and any other kind of "centrism" including humanism and anthropocentrism, although I have not been conscious or critical of it for long. I became more conscious of it, however—albeit somewhat vaguely—during my graduate study at the University of California, Berkeley, in the early 1980s, whenever I asked the question, "What has brought me here to the United States to study?" This nagging question stared me in the face, but I shied away from confronting it, like an ostrich burying its head in the sand. As a Korean political theorist, however, I began to tackle the subject of Western-centrism (i.e., the idea or practice of placing the West at the center of one's worldview) in a more serious manner when I spent my first sabbatical year at Harvard in 1995-96. After my return to Korea in 1996, I continued my immersion in the study of Western-centrism in a more systematic way. My research culminated in the publication of a book entitled *Seogujungsimjuuireul Neomeoseo* (Beyond the Shadow of Western-centrism) in 2004. The book would be later published by Lexington with some adaptations as *Western-centrism and Contemporary Korean Political Thought* (2015).

It is interesting to observe the shift in the terminology I used to refer to the supremacy and dominance of Western civilization as my research progressed. In the beginning I chose to use the word *Eurocentrism*, following the general Western convention, then I switched to *Westcentrism*, and finally I have settled on *Western-centrism*. The reasons I prefer *Western-centrism* to *Eurocentrism* is the former includes the United States, Canada, and Australia more explicitly than the latter and it is the United States now exercising a globally preeminent influence in most areas of human life, notably politics, the economy, the military, and mass culture. Despite this shift in the use of terms, it should be noted that the concept they refer to remains almost the same. Thus, various chapters based on previously published essays are not consistent in the use of the words referring to Western supremacy, but I decided to leave such differences intact to preserve the history of my own usage.

While dealing with the subject of Western-centrism, I also engaged with comparative political theory (philosophy). In the concluding chapter of *Seogujungsimjuuireul Neomeoseo* I suggested comparative political theory as one of the promising strategies to counter Western-centrism prevalent in political theory. As a matter of fact, in addition to my serious preoccupation with the study of Western-centrism, a series of developments surrounding my academic life stimulated my serious engagement with comparative political theory.

First, the creation of the Korean Political Thought Association by Korean political theorists in 1996 would provide a vital forum in which Korean political theorists specializing variously in Eastern and Western political theory as well as in ancient and modern historical periods met together, and the hybridization of various political theories across times and spaces began to take place among members. Second, my organization of a small study group called the "East-West Political Theory Seminar" with my graduate students at Sogang University in early 1998 would offer fertile ground for the keen interest in comparative political theory that began to germinate among my graduate students and me. In the seminar we usually read and discussed classics in political thought including Western political theorists such as Plato, Aristotle, Machiavelli, Hobbes, Locke, Rousseau, M. Wollstonecraft, Burke, de Tocqueville, J. S. Mill, and Marx; Chinese thinkers such as Confucius, Mencius, Laozi, Xunzi, Han Fei Tzu, and Zhu Xi; and some Korean thinkers such as Yi I, Jeong Yakyong, and Yu Gil-jun. It was rewarding to observe that some of my graduate students wrote their master's and doctoral theses from the perspective of comparative political theory, taking advantage of such intellectual engagement.

Third and last, I must mention my appointment to the editorial committee of *Korea Journal*–a quarterly academic journal published by the Korean National Commission for UNESCO–from 1999 to 2007. To be frank, little did I dream that I, a professor of a certain generation who was tenured comfortably and complacently at a Korean university in the 1990s, would ever write English papers or books. Of course, there were some notable Korean political scientists who wrote and published their articles and papers in overseas journals, but this was usually confined to those specializing in South and North Korean politics, political process focusing on quantitative analysis such as voting behavior, and international relations related to Korea and East Asia. Given that political theory deals with more abstract and supposedly more difficult and profound issues of a normative kind, most Korean political theorists residing in Korea at the time shied away from producing their work in English–unless they had been educated in English in their precollege years and thus were able to use English like native speakers. I was not one of the exceptions. However, as I worked on the editorial committee of *Korea Journal*, I began to seriously consider taking that opportunity to publish my work in English. Incidentally, as a visiting professor at the Harvard-Yenching Institute, I had presented a paper at a colloquium of the Korea Institute in early May 1996. The paper criticized one of Samuel P. Huntington's important arguments in *The Third Wave* (1991) that Confucian democracy is a contradiction in terms. The argument was made in a sweeping way when he examined the status of democracy in East Asia. While trying to refute his contention point by point and demonstrate that Confucianism and democracy are compatible, I was unconsciously engaged in comparative political theory or a cross-cultural dialogue by which I examined Confucianism in light of democracy and, in turn, democracy from the perspective of Confucianism. I expanded and revised the paper to publish it under the title "Confucianism and Democracy in East Asia: A Critique of Samuel P. Huntington's *Third Wave*" in *Korea Journal* (Autumn 1999). Such was the way in which I began to engage in comparative political theory and publish my academic work in English.

I have written fourteen papers in English and have published eleven since 1999. But a considerable number of them were adapted for inclusion in my books *Western-centrism and Contemporary Korean*

Political Thought (2015) and *Contemporary Korean Political Thought and Park Chung-hee* (forthcoming in 2017). To publish this book, I selected five published articles and two unpublished papers. Chapter 2 on the cultural identity of East Asia is an English translation of my Korean essay published in 2003, and Chapter 5 on *Datong* (大同) democracy is based on my paper I presented at an international conference held in Hong Kong last year. The influence of my affiliation with *Korea Journal* is shown vividly by the fact that four of the seven chapters are based on papers published previously in the journal.

I have to point out that the papers in this book are not necessarily the work of comparative political theory. Chapters on Richard Kim's novel *The Martyred* and Rousseau's political thought are such examples. But they fit into the subtitle of the book, "A Journey across Ideological Times and Spaces," so I have included them. Finally, although comparative political theory is the overarching theme in this book, I shall not give a detailed explanation of comparative political theory here in the Preface/Acknowledgments, since the introductory Chapter 1 on comparative political philosophy will give readers some useful clues and the following chapters will illustrate how to practice comparative political theory.

Now is the time to acknowledge my intellectual and personal debts to those who guided and helped my journey toward writing these essays and publishing them in a book. Needless to say, I am soberly aware of my invaluable intellectual debts to numerous thinkers and academics, alive or dead, who have shaped and influenced my academic self throughout my intellectual journey. But I have to acknowledge my academic debts to two late professors of political theory in particular, for two chapters in the book: the essay on *The Martyred* (Chapter 7) and the one on Rousseau (Chapter 6). The original draft for Chapter 7 on *The Martyred* was written and submitted as the term paper in the graduate seminar "Politics and Literature" at Berkeley, which the late professor Norman Jacobson gave in the winter-spring quarters of 1983, now almost thirty-five years ago. I was deeply engaged with the theme of the seminar, politics and truth, analyzing Richard E. Kim's novel *The Martyred* in its light. Professor Jacobson was always an inspiring and generous teacher who showed inexhaustible patience while listening to my inchoate ideas, conveyed with stammering English. Although I was happy to be reunited with him at Berkeley in 2004, I was very sorry to hear that he passed away a few years later in 2007. I want to dedicate this chapter to the memory of Professor Jacobson, a great teacher.

The publication of my article on Rousseau in *Interpretation: A Journal of Political Philosophy* (2012) is greatly indebted to the late Professor Hilail Gildin. My encounter with Professor Gildin was quite unusual and contingent, and thus I shall tell the story here. In Western scholarship, the mainstream interpretation of Rousseau's view of political participation has been negative or passive regarding the question of whether his citizens are allowed active political participation such as discussion and debate. In my doctoral dissertation on political participation submitted in 1987, I suggested my own interpretation in support of active participation, criticizing the mainstream interpretation. After receiving my Ph.D., however, I did not have the opportunity to develop my views into a full-fledged paper for a long time. Meanwhile, I came across Gildin's outstanding book, *Rousseau's Social Contract* (1985), without knowing him very well, and found that he was one of the few scholars who supported an activist interpretation of political participation in Rousseau's political thought with a more elaborate argument, confirming my position.

Taking time out to complete a paper on Rousseau in early 2010 and planning to present it at the annual conference of the Midwest Political Science Association in March 31-April 3, 2011, I sent it to Professor Gildin by e-mail, hoping to receive some comment (if any at all) from him on my paper, even though I was an obscure scholar. Although I was in broad agreement with his argument, which also influenced my own paper with his inspiring interpretation and broad-brush approach, I still felt that his argument needed more closely knit reasoning and a thorough examination of Rousseau's other writings to overwhelm the prevalent mainstream interpretation. On behalf of his interpretation, I took up such a task, meticulously reviewing and criticizing recent versions of the mainstream interpretation and adducing further strong textual evidences to strengthen the activist interpretation. After reading my paper and giving some complimentary comments a few months later, Professor Gildin suggested that it be published in *Interpretation*. Of course, his offer was a surprising great luck I could not refuse. So it was published in a 2012 issue of that journal. (After the publication I found out he was the journal's editor-in-chief, but at the time I did not know of its existence, not to mention its reputation.) Recently, I tried to contact Professor Gildin to get permission to publish the article in this book;

however, I was very sorry to hear he had passed away on March 4, 2015. Exactly two years after his death, I now acknowledge my sincere gratitude to the late Professor Gildin for his generosity in publishing my article in *Interpretation*, expressing my deep sorrow for his death and great admiration for his academic fellowship, which seemed to transcend any petty scholarly differences. So the chapter on Rousseau is dedicated to him in memory of his academic generosity and our tacit friendship.

Now, it is my very great pleasure to acknowledge the invaluable support and help I received in the process of publishing this book. First of all, I have to acknowledge that I was able to write new chapters and edit previously published articles for this book with the generous support of the National Research Foundation of Korea Grant funded by the Korean government (NRF-2014S1A3A2043763). I was also fortunate enough to receive the 2016 Sogang University Research Grant (201610048.01) and the 2017 Sogang SK Supex Fund, both of which provided financial support at the final stage of the preparation and publication of this book.

Professor Wu Chan Je of Korean Literature, director of the Sogang University Press, was enthusiastic about this book project. He was very instrumental in its publication by the Sogang University Press, administratively as well as financially. I also appreciate Professor Christopher C. Robinson at Clarkson University for his unfailing support for my academic work and his timely provision of valuable information. In addition, I always feel thankful to lawyer Simon S. Hong, a longtime friend of mine from my graduate years at Berkeley, for his enduring friendship and warm encouragement of my academic journey.

Many people helped me with the task of English translation and other editorial and publishing tasks. First and foremost, I have to acknowledge, among others, Lynne Jensen Lampe's sincere and patient editorial work for this book, as she did with my previous one, *Contemporary Korean Political Thought and Park Chung-hee* (forthcoming). I feel really lucky and happy to have an editor like Lynne, who recently joined in my long journey as a travelling companion. I am also grateful to Lee Jong Won, my research assistant and a master's student at Sogang University. He transcribed all published articles from PDF format to text files by first converting and then editing all of them, to facilitate further revision and editing. He also examined the whole manuscript chapter by chapter, particularly checking citations and the references and filing index entries with great care. It has been a great pleasure to meet such a sincere and bright graduate student as Jong Won. Finally, I appreciate my two graduate students, each of whom coauthored an article with me, for giving their generous permission to publish them in this book: Lee Ji Yun coauthored the article for Chapter 1 and Eom Kwanyong, the article for Chapter 4.

Article-length versions (though all revised and adapted here) of five of the chapters have been published previously in English, and I am grateful for permission to draw on them.

Chapter 1 is based on "Seeking Comparative Political Philosophy from an East Asian Perspective: A Transversal Cross-

Cultural Dialogue," *Korea Journal* 53:3 (Autumn 2013), 78-102 (coauthored with Lee Ji Yun), with permission from the Korean National Commission for UNESCO.

Chapter 3 is based on "The Rule of Law and the Rule of Virtue: On the Necessity for Their Mutual Integration," *Korea Journal* 43:1 (Spring 2003), 234-60, with permission from the Korean National Commission for UNESCO.

Chapter 4 is based on "Comparative Analysis of Eastern and Western Tyranny: Focusing on Aristotle and Mencius," *Korea Journal* 43:4 (Winter 2003), 113-36 (coauthored with Eom Kwanyong), with permission from the Korean National Commission for UNESCO.

Chapter 6 is based on "Reexamining Rousseau's Political Thought: Does Citizens' Political Participation Include Public Discussions and Debates?" *Interpretation* 39:2 (Spring/Summer 2012), 139-63, with permission from *Interpretation: A Journal of Political Philosophy* (Timothy W. Burns, editor-in-chief).

Chapter 7 is based on "Politics and Truth: An Analysis of Richard E. Kim's Novel, *The Martyred*," *Korea Journal* 47:2 (Summer 2007), 184-207, with permission from the Korean National Commission for UNESCO.

Jung In Kang
Seoul
March 2017

Chapter 1

Comparative Political Philosophy from an East Asian Perspective: A Transversal Cross-Cultural Dialogue

In today's era of rapid globalization, comparative political philosophy is more important than ever before, and yet, as Fred Dallmayr (1999, 1-2) observed a long time ago, "comparative political theory or philosophy is either completely non-existent or at best an embryonic and marginalized type of endeavor."[1] This chapter presents a speculative exploration of comparative political philosophy from an East Asian perspective.[2] In order to overcome the abiding Western-centrism[3] of the world, East Asian intellectuals must enact a comparative political philosophy by actively reinterpreting and reappropriating traditional political thought. There are three reasons

1 See also Kang Jung In (1999, 2000, 2003) and Kang Jung In and Eom Kwanyong (2003).

2 Of course, this is not to say that comparative political theory from other national or regional perspectives is not equally important or desirable.

3 I use the term *Western-centrism* instead of the more common *Eurocentrism* in order to explicitly include European civilizations that have developed in non-European territories (e.g., the United States, Canada, Australia). Moreover, since the Second World War, the United States has surpassed Europe to become the primary nation setting the terms and agenda of global politics.

why this is necessary and possible. First, the traditional political philosophy of East Asia (i.e., China, Korea, and Japan)[4] is potentially compatible (or commensurable) with Western political philosophy, owing to its basis in the common values of humanity, and this compatibility must be retrieved and secured. Second, to make an ecological analogy, the legacy of East Asian political philosophy must be cultivated and expanded for the sake of "biodiversity" because East Asian civilization offers precious potential and actual resources (including political philosophy) that are not available in Western civilization. Third, East Asians are in a strategic position to effectively develop this legacy, because it constitutes part of their identity and is therefore more familiar to them.

This chapter will first diagnose the objective conditions of today's world that are helping to displace the hegemony of Western-centrism with polycentrism. Then, it will suggest the proper guidelines for deconstructing Western-centrism and engaging in comparative political philosophy by examining the ideas of transversality, cross-cultural dialogue, and biological analogies.

4 Samuel P. Huntington (1996, 45) distinguishes the Sinic (Chinese) civilization from the Japanese. But in this chapter, *East Asia* refers broadly to China, Korea, and Japan, which are linked by the strong influence of Confucianism on their political philosophy, even though each nation has a distinct cultural tradition. East Asia often includes Vietnam as well. For commonalities and regional differences in East Asia, see Murphey (2010, 1-19) and Fairbank, Reischauer, and Craig (1989, 1-16). In the next section, however, when I examine the prospect for a polycentric world, the overall economic power of the East Asian region becomes more relevant, so I expand the connotation of *East Asia* to include the countries belonging to the Association of Southeast Asian Nations (ASEAN).

Toward a Polycentric World

An examination of contemporary life reveals that Western-centrism is being steadily supplanted by polycentrism, thereby enabling transversal and cross-cultural (or cross-civilizational) dialogue and allowing for a more equal comparative political philosophy between the "West" and the "Rest."[5]

First and foremost, I would like to note the development of globalization, which is making people realize the vital necessity of acknowledging the ascendancy of the indivisible global common good. It is now widely accepted that all the people of the world must work collectively to address various global issues, including the possible extermination of humanity through nuclear war, the responsibility for saving the ecosystem from great peril, the international guarantee of human rights, the improvement of social and economic conditions for the world's poor, and so on. We may also add the viability of a global economy that has greatly benefitted from this increased interactivity, yet is simultaneously threatened by it. Indeed, we are still in the midst of one of the worst global economic depressions in history, rooted in the breakdown of the US financial system and its uncontrollable and

5 Stuart Hall (1992, 279) stressed the world's Eurocentrism by titling one of his articles "The West and the Rest," using the term *Rest* to refer to the non-West, although both are synonymous and residual categories. In addition to East Asian civilizations, the Rest includes Islamic, Indian, Southeast Asian, Latin American, African, and other civilizations, all of which have been forced to address the serious problem of Western-centrism. For more on this problem in social sciences, see UNESCO and ISSC, *World Social Science Report: Knowledge Divides* (Paris: UNESCO Publishing, 2010), which examines the wide variations of the problem of Eurocentrism in diverse regions.

unpredictable worldwide chain reaction. All of these issues demand the acknowledgment of an indivisible global common good. As Peter Taylor (2000, 68) points out, with the advent of globalization, "We have moved from the optimistic situation when the 'goods' of modernity were promised to all to the pessimistic situation with the 'bads' of modernity threatening all."

No individual state, however large and powerful, can ever hope to enact the indivisible global common good by itself, which is why all nations are increasingly aware of the need for international cooperation. As such, the concept of "global" has become synonymous with "universal," meaning "for all of humanity." This global consciousness represents a radical challenge to the dominance of Western civilization, presaging the fundamental subversion of Western-centrism.

Another auspicious sign that Western-centrism is being displaced is the recent strong economic performance by non-Western regions and nations–for example, East Asia (notably China), Brazil, India, and Russia. Over the last two or three hundred years, many non-Western societies have tried to match the political and economic strength of the West in order to grow out of Western-centrism. Thus, they have been forced to play the game of modernization, which was designed to disadvantage them from the beginning. In other words, in order to develop more effective strategies to counter Western-centrism, non-Western societies must first accommodate Western-centrism by adopting Western political and economic strategies. Once non-Western nations have attained political and economic parity with the West, they may begin to demand the revision of the rules of the

Western-centric game, but until then, they must struggle to survive by conforming to the biased rules set by the West. In relationships marked by dominance, the weaker party must acquiesce to the rules set by the dominant party, putting itself at a disadvantage, and prove its ability according to these rules. In the process of modernization, non-Western societies have been forced into this type of no-win situation and have unwittingly internalized Western-centrism.

Of course, we must never deny the significance of the monocentric military dominance of Western civilization, as exemplified by the recent conflicts in Iraq, Afghanistan, and Libya, led by the United States and its allies. Nevertheless, the dynamic economic growth of East Asia, Brazil, Russia, and India represents a definitive long-term shift toward polycentrism. Economic trends over the last three decades confirm this, as seen in the following table, which shows what percentage of the global gross national income (GNI) was represented by the individual GNI of major states (and state confederations) in the years 1980, 2000, and 2010.

Table 1. *Percentage of the GNI by Region*

	1980	2000	2010
World	100	100	100
EU	33.8	28.4	27.36
China	1.9	3.6	9.1
China (including Hong Kong and Macao)	2.1	4.2	9.5
Japan	11.0	13.6	8.6
South Korea	0.6	1.4	1.6
China + Japan + South Korea	13.7	19.3	19.7

ASEAN	1.6	1.9	2.6
China (including Hong Kong and Macao) + Japan + South Korea + ASEAN	15.3	21.0	22.3
USA	25.9	30.6	23.4
Canada	2.5	2.1	2.3
Mexico	1.5	1.8	1.6
North America	29.9	34.5	27.3
Brazil	2.3	2.1	2.9
India	1.7	1.4	2.5
Russia	-	0.8	2.3
Brazil + India + Russia	4.0	4.3	7.7

Source: World Bank (http://data.world.bank).

Note: The figures are rounded to one decimal place. For the year 2000, the combined individual ratios of China, Japan, South Korea, and ASEAN differ slightly from the cumulative ratio of those regions, because the relative ratio was slightly different when weighed against the total global GNI. For the years 1980 and 2000, the total for the EU represents the cumulative total of the individual GNIs of the 27 member states of the EU as of 2010. For this table, the ASEAN total does not include Myanmar, because relevant data were not available. The GNI of Brunei in 2010 is not available and was thus excluded. No data were available from 1980 for Vietnam, Laos, Russia, Macao, and Cambodia. The data for Hong Kong in 1980 are based on GDP rather than GNI.

According to Table 1, in 1980 the GNI of East Asia (including China, Japan, South Korea, and the ASEAN) was 15.3% of the global total, whereas that of North America was 29.9% and that of the European Union (EU) was 33.8%. In 2010, however, two years after the global financial crisis began in the United States, the GNI of East Asia had risen to 22.3% of the global total, whereas that of North America was 27.3% and that of the EU was 27.4%. Thus, the relative weight of East Asia in the total global GNI increased by an impressive 7%, whereas the total for Brazil, India, and Russia also made a strong showing, rising from 4.0% to 7.7%. The EU has seen a rather sharp decrease of 6.4%, although the decline since 2000 has only been about 1.0%. Since 1980, North America's overall decline of 2.6% has been rather moderate, but the 7.2% drop since 2000 is much more considerable. That 7.2% drop comes almost entirely from the United States, which also fell off by 7.2% from 2000 to 2010. In that same period, China enjoyed a phenomenal increase of 5.5% (from 3.6% to 9.1%), overtaking Japan, which declined from 13.6% in 2000 to 8.6% in 2010. In fact, if not for Japan's loss of 5%, the total GNI of East Asia in 2010 would have equaled or surpassed that of the EU and North America.[6]

The coincidence of the relative economic decline of the United States and the phenomenal growth of China's economy and military spending has led to the proliferation of the "China threat" theory and the term *G-2* (Group of Two). Although no one can predict how the global political order will be shaped in the long run, the world is undeniably shifting towards polycentrism with the rise of East Asia (especially China), Brazil, India, and Russia.

6 For reference, "In 1960, the aggregate GNP of Japan and East Asia came to no more than 4% of that of the global total, while that of North America (i.e., United States, Canada, and Mexico) was 37%" (Kang Jung In 2004, 502). Of course, GNP is measured differently from GNI.

Transversality

Any attempt to deconstruct Western-centrism must transcend the Western view, which observes the world in terms of binary oppositions (e.g., subject and object, reason and emotion, mind and body, West and non-West) and then privileges one of the two sides. In order to avoid the trap of focusing solely on isolated differences and diversity, we can turn to the concept of transversality, which fundamentally challenges Western universalism. The term *transversality*[7] has been taken up by various postmodern theorists, including Calvin O. Schrag, Félix Guattari, and Jung Hwa Yol. Applying their theories in an attempt to characterize global citizenship, Lee Dong-su described transversality as follows:

> Transversality aims to formulate a series of solidary, collective commonalities from the traversing and crossing communications among individuals, while still preserving their identities. The goals of transversality are to enhance communicability between individualities, to build sympathy and mutual understanding, and to simultaneously cultivate diversity and commonality, while maintaining individualities. (Lee Dong-su 2010, 183)

7 In mathematics, *transversal* is defined as a line that cuts through two or more other lines. Jean-Paul Sartre first used the concept of transversality in a philosophical context in his 1934 essay, *La Transcendance de l'ego: Esquisse d'une description phénomenologique* (The Transcendence of the Ego: An Existentialist Theory of Consciousness), and the concept was later developed by Gilles Deleuze and Félix Guattari.

In my discussion of transversality, I rely upon recent works by Jung Hwa Yol, who has extensively applied the term in the field of political philosophy while attempting to deconstruct Western-centrism. Jung (1995, 15) declares that transversality is the "crossroads of truth across the boundaries of different cultures; it is the way of thinking about truth cross-culturally." In order to apply the concept of transversality properly, we must first examine its implications for comparative political theory.

First of all, the concept of transversality exposes the universalism of modernity as an embodiment of Western-centrism, thus articulating the problematique of Western-centrism. No political theory can have any privilege of truth, for there is no such thing as a universal political theory that embraces all political theories.[8] Therefore, no political theory—past or present, Eastern or Western—can make a monopolistic claim on inclusive universality. Instead, it is essential to forge a transversal connectivity by recognizing and incorporating different voices from divergent cultures and societies. Furthermore, communicability and integration must be actively enhanced in order to preserve such diversity.

Second, transversality does not present non-Western political theory as the alternative to Western political theory, though it recognizes the differences between the two. Certainly, there will always be differences that cannot be sutured by universalism, but the world cannot make real progress so long as such differences are simply established and entrenched, with no communication. Transversality

8 This is adapted from Maurice Merleau-Ponty's remark: "There is not a philosophy which contains all philosophies" (quoted in Jung Hwa Yol 1999, 277).

refuses to either ignore differences or totalize them into a single whole. The recognition of diversity that is inherent in transversality is not intended simply to identify differences, but to transfigure them. Jung's concept of transversality involves interacting with diversity in order to reform something during a stage of transition. The goal is to complement "what is lacking or deficient in one . . . by the other," thereby enacting a "self-transfiguring process of one's encounter with the Other and becoming another being" (Jung Hwa Yol 2009a, 432).

Third, transversality avoids several fallacies that have hindered other attempts to overcome Western-centrism. Non-Western attempts to deconstruct reductive Western universalism tend to stress differences from the West, thereby reinforcing the supposed primacy and ascendency of the West and reproducing the binary oppositions embedded in Western-centrism. Any dichotomy that emphasizes the West and non-West can only ever be an assimilative or reverse model (i.e., reverse Orientalism) that inevitably bestows universality upon one of the two. Transversality, however, informs us that cultures are always plural and that genuine global cultures can only emerge when each culture is encouraged to maintain its own indigenous roots while actively engaging with other cultures. That is, cultures must develop through transversal mediation with one another. From this perspective, Western-centrism can only be supplanted by interrogating both Eastern and Western political theories from a broader perspective that incorporates cultures from different places and time periods.

According to Jung, the concept of transversality opens up the horizon to overcome the "polarizing dichotomies" of universality and particularity, identity and difference, and the West and non-

West and "advances the cause of cross-cultural fertilization or hybridization as well as cross-disciplinary engagement in which truth as communicability privileges, and is monopolized by, neither the West nor philosophy alone" (Jung Hwa Yol 2009b, 28-29)

However, as a non-Western scholar, I have some lingering questions, perhaps even dogged skepticism, regarding postmodernist discourses–including those on transversality–that stress the need to recognize and acknowledge the differences of the Other. Given that Western-centrism tends to ignore those differences, any added emphasis would seem to be a positive development, but I believe this view often serves to reinforce the Western perspective. In fact, models that privilege difference merely for the sake of difference inevitably evoke a rather ludicrous situation by encouraging people to overlook universal problems. For instance, what are Westerners to do about the harsh authoritarian regimes, rampant political corruption, and patriarchal oppression of women that are commonly found in non-Western countries? Of course, all of those problems are also embedded in Western culture, but does that mean that Westerners should abstain from criticizing them out of respect for the different cultures of the Other?

Furthermore, non-Westerners have learned, either voluntarily or forcibly, not only to recognize but also to respect the distinctive aspects of Western civilization–the West's Enlightenment, reason and philosophy, liberalism, democracy, feminism, science and technology, industrialism and capitalism, and so on–in the name of universality. But while Western exceptionalism has privileged these cultural elements as superior, the distinctive aspects of Eastern culture are typically dismissed as inferior and deviant according to Orientalism. In other words, attempts to simply respect one another's differences will forever be unbalanced, unless Western culture begins to show greater respect for non-Western cultures and non-Western respect for Western culture becomes demystified to a certain extent.[9] Thus, following only the suggestions offered by the concept of transversality, non-Westerners may never be able to recognize and acknowledge their differences from the West on an equal footing, although the acceptance of Western universality is clearly and gradually receding in the postmodern world.

In reconsidering the nature of universality, Immanuel Wallerstein's examination of the supposed universalism of European social science may yield some insight:

> European social science was resolutely universalist in asserting

9 In my discussion, there are two critical points with regard to postmodernist discourses of difference and otherness. The first point criticizing cultural relativism has been widely addressed in Western literature, but to my knowledge, the second point criticizing the imbalance between the West and the Rest in terms of their respect for each other's differences has not been critically addressed. For example, take the need for heteronomy (ethics of focusing on the Other) that is stressed by Emmanuel Levinas, particularly his ethical philosophy of dialogue and responsibility on the primacy of the other (Levinas 1999, 97-109). His philosophy is primarily applicable to dominant groups (e.g., Western society, whites, males, the upper class, Christians), because marginalized groups (e.g., non-Western society, nonwhites, females, the working class, people of non-Christian religions) are already well-versed in the ethics of heteronomy. Indeed, whereas heteronomy is imposed on the latter groups each and every day, for the former groups it is simply an optional virtue, a postmodern variant of the "white man's burden." Kwame Anthony Appiah commits a similar error when he defines the "second strand of cosmopolitanism" as the "recognition that human beings are different and that we can learn from each other's differences" (Appiah 2006, 4) without seriously considering the imbalance of power that is inherent between diverse groups.

> that whatever it was that happened in Europe in the sixteenth to nineteenth centuries represented a pattern that was applicable everywhere, either because it was a progressive achievement of mankind which was irreversible or because it represented the fulfillment of humanity's basic needs via the removal of artificial obstacles to this realization. What you saw now in Europe was not only good but the face of the future everywhere. (Wallerstein 1997, 96-97)

As a social scientist who is well acquainted with the bewildering diversity and multiplicity in today's social world, I do not agree with Wallerstein's use of *universal* to mean "equally applying and as a matter of principle everywhere in the universe" (Lummis 2002, 69), a definition better suited to scientific truths or Hegelian idealist philosophies. However, the reason the universalist claim of European social science was plausible is well explained by Wallerstein (1997). The reason, he suggested, is a Western unilinear progressive view of history with European supremacy (i.e., that the progressive development of humanity has been overshadowed by the achievements of modern Europe, which were forcibly implanted in the Rest later on). Hence comes the emergence of the universality of European social science, and thus the task of Europeanization (or Westernization) is thrust upon the "inferior" non-West.

In other words, the principal ideas and values representing the progress of the world–democracy, liberalism, capitalism, human rights, and enlightenment rationality–are purported to have originated exclusively in the West, so that other civilizations were basically forced to pursue those ideals as their desirable end (*telos*).

Western civilization was placed in a superior position by being granted these original (genetic) and teleological privileges. As a result, non-Western societies had no choice but to take Western civilization as their reference point and pursue Westernization in the name of modernization.

The supposed universality of European social science seems to rely upon and derive from the genetic and teleological privileges of Western civilization, rather than from the superiority of its scientific method or logical reasoning. Thus, the universality of Western civilization in general and Western social science in particular is not a universality of scientific knowledge (universal truth) but rather a hegemony (consensus); that is, moral and intellectual plausibility.

This point also applies to the universal values of Western modern civilization. Today, we accept human rights as universal values, not in the sense that they are valid across all of time and space, but in the sense that they are *prevalent over all* or *widely applicable.* Human rights were developed as European universal values in conjunction with the emergence of capitalism and the sovereign state, which monopolized the legitimate use of violence. However, they cannot be reasonably claimed as valid across all of time and space. For example, the provision that "[n]o one shall be subjected to arbitrary arrest" (Universal Declaration of Human Rights, article 9) would have no meaning in a society that has no police or prisons. In the same way, the "right to form and to join trade unions" (Universal Declaration of Human Rights, article 23.4) will serve no purpose in a society whose economy is not based on wage labor. Such rights would not have been useful in an African tribal society or in sixteenth-century Korea, where capitalism was unheard of. The idea that human rights are universal values in the contemporary world (in the sense that they are "widely applicable") derives solely from the fact that most non-Western societies have now adopted capitalism and the sovereign-state system (i.e., a program of capitalist industrialization under the auspices of a sovereign-state government) by way of colonialism, imperialism, violent conquest (or its threat), or rational persuasion.[10]

In other words, the West has effectively transformed the reality of non-Western societies into the Western style by transplanting and generalizing Western institutions and practices (e.g., sovereign states and capitalism) all over the world. As a result, non-Western societies have come to accept the values and ideas that are necessary for Western civilization (e.g., democracy, freedom of the press) as universal values and ideas. This shows the hegemonic, ex post facto process by which much of Western modernity has become universalized. In this sense, Western modernity may be universal, but only in the sense that it is prevalent over all or widely applicable. Rather than universal truth, modernity represents a hegemonic consensus–prima facie universality–which is always subject to revision according to temporal and spatial contexts.

Returning to the relevance of transversality for comparative political theory, theorists of transversality have not yet advanced a concrete and viable methodology of how to engage comparative political philosophy transversally. However, their theories point to cross-cultural dialogue among different cultures and civilizations. In the next section, I will focus on cross-cultural dialogue and then

10 For my discussion in this paragraph, I am indebted to Lummis (2002, 67-68).

suggest some biological analogies that might indicate the proper method for comparative political theory.

Cross-Cultural Dialogue

Various theories of multiculturalism have been enthusiastically advanced within Western academia. Within the liberal tradition, liberal universalism (Barry 2001) and liberal multiculturalism (notably, Kymlicka 1989, 1995) occupy opposite poles, while outside the tradition, value pluralism (Gray 1995, 1998) competes with interactive multiculturalism (Parekh 2006). Notably, however, the theories of both liberal universalism and liberal multiculturalism are founded on the conviction that takes liberalism as universal in principle, which explains why they have acquired prima facie plausibility within Western nations where liberalism is accepted as the universal frame. However, in order to conduct a cross-cultural and transversal dialogue in comparative political theory at the global level, the universality of liberalism should not be taken for granted, for such an assumption will be susceptible to claims of Western-centrism. Thus, Bhikhu Parekh's interactive multiculturalism, which does not presuppose the universality of liberalism, merits serious examination. The idea of cross-cultural dialogue that I outline in this chapter largely relies on his work.

According to Parekh, as different groups of people develop their own living capacities and seek the meaning and significance of human life, they create distinct varieties of culture. Although all people share some common capacities, those capacities are differently defined and developed by their distinct cultures. As such, culture mediates human universality. It is impossible for any one individual culture to thoroughly realize the full range of human possibilities, and in most cases, a culture will focus more intently on some capacities and sensibilities while neglecting or marginalizing others. Therein lies the reason cross-cultural dialogue is needed. To a greater or lesser degree, each of us must function within the boundaries of our own culture, which has developed in a particular way. Contact and exchange with other cultures inevitably allow us to deepen and enrich our knowledge and understanding of our own culture while also providing welcome opportunities to borrow and integrate attractive aspects of other cultures into our own. Accordingly, cross-cultural dialogue is an essential condition for the flourishing of human life (Parekh 1998, 212-13).

Parekh (2008, 156-57) notes that culture is not static but composed of heterogeneous strands and differing interpretations that are constantly competing with one another. Indeed, this inherent heterogeneity and mutability is what allows us to incorporate elements of other cultures into our own through cross-cultural dialogue. In light of this idea, Parekh urges us to abandon the notion of liberalism as a fixed doctrine in favor of free intellectual exploration, deconstructing liberalism into a set of principles or values and accepting only those that are relevant when combined with values from other cultures. In fact, he regards his theory of multiculturalism as an example of such an exploration, wherein he approves of certain liberal values (e.g., human dignity, equality, critical rationality, respect for others, and tolerance) but reinterprets them with reference to other cultures. For instance, he endorses rationality, but in a persuasive and conversational form rather than an argumentative and combative form. He cherishes individuality, while recognizing our cultural embeddedness, and he stresses that any universal values we may have are inherently mediated through particular cultures (Parekh 2006, 368-69).

Parekh coined the term *interactive multiculturalism* for this theory, which is the result of his intercultural experimentation. This method of intercultural experimentation may be called *interculturalism*, defined by an emphasis on respect for other cultures, the heterogeneity and fluidity of cultures, and the importance of intercultural dialogue.[11] Parekh illustrates the method of interculturalism by examining the thoughts of Mahatma Gandhi. According to Parekh, Gandhi was born into an orthodox Hindu family and was educated in the Hindu tradition. Later, he went to England and South Africa, where he learned about Christianity, Judaism, and other Western thought, and began to critically question his own tradition. Gandhi had long supported the Hindu idea of *ahimsa* (nonviolence), but after encountering Christian thought and practice, he realized that the Hindu idea was too passive, in that it merely sought to avoid harming others while taking no active interest in their well-being. Thus, he adopted the "socially oriented Christian

11 Parekh (2006, 372) explicitly refers to his theory as "creative and interactive multiculturalism" but does not give a specific term to his theoretical method, which is marked by transgressing established boundaries, borrowing from other cultures, and combining elements from different cultures. He only mentions "intercultural experimentation" when illustrating this method with his account of Gandhi (Parekh 2006, 370).

concept of *caritas*" or *agape* (God's divine love for humanity) and "integrated it with the Hindu concept of non-violence, and arrived at the idea of the active service of all living beings inspired by the principle of universal love" (Parekh 2006, 371). Gandhi also felt that "Christian *caritas* was excessively emotional" and could thus imperil internal calmness and emotional self-sufficiency, so he "reinterpreted and revised it in the light of the Hindu concept of non-attachment (*anasakti*)" (Parekh 2006, 371). By interrogating the Hindu concept of nonviolence from a Christian perspective and reinterpreting the Christian concept of *caritas* from a Hindu perspective, Gandhi propagated the "novel idea of an active and positive but detached and non-emotive universal love" (Parekh 2006, 371). His hybridization of Hinduism, Christianity, and liberalism represented a cross-cultural dialogue, or transversal comparison, between "different moral, religious, and cultural traditions," through which he "destabilized settled identities and created new ones" (Parekh 2006, 372).

For another example of how cross-cultural dialogue can provide a method for comparative political theory, we can critically compare the concept of human rights in modern liberalism and the concept of human relationships put forth by traditional Confucianism. Any political community should guarantee a minimum of human dignity for its members, including the right to subsistence, although this perquisite may be differential and discriminatory. Somewhere beyond the horizon of this primordial problematique, the differing approaches of "human rights" and "human relationships" encounter one another. A comparative study of political theory based on cross-cultural dialogue would inevitably require the human relationships approach to justify itself in light of individual freedom and equality, and as a result, the negative aspects of the approach would be accordingly reformulated. In contrast, such a study would point out that the human rights approach neglects the care and responsibility for others, as stressed by the human relationships approach, and must therefore adapt itself to address some of the problems that can arise from "rights talk," such as the breakdown of community, the loss of authority, and atomistic and isolated individualism. A cross-cultural dialogue recommended by comparative political theory does not aim to construct a parallel layout of Eastern and Western political theories, but rather seeks to achieve a confluence between the two. Such a comparative work could pioneer a new hybrid political theory transcending both Western-centrism and East Asian particularism.

Cross-cultural dialogue is the key to successfully traversing East and West and overcoming Western-centrism. When working on a comparative political theory from an East Asian perspective, cross-cultural dialogue can help us reach an expanding and evolving consensus. In the first stage, we must critically question Western thought from the perspective of East Asian thought, and vice versa, in order to lay the foundation for a mutual consensus by identifying their affinities and differences. Then in the second stage, on the basis of this initial work, we will engage in more intensive exchange related to the areas of conflict and dissent, thereby expanding the preliminary consensus. Charles Taylor makes a similar point in his article, "Conditions of an Unforced Consensus on Human Rights":

> This is the situation at the outset, in any case, when consensus

> on some aspect of human rights has just been attained. Later a process can follow of mutual learning, moving toward a "fusion of horizon" in Gadamer's term, in which the moral universe of the other becomes less strange. Out of this will come further borrowings and the creation of new hybrid forms. (Taylor 1999, 136)

Cross-cultural dialogue is not only applicable to different cultures (e.g., East and West), but also to the past and the present. Due to modernization (Westernization), non-Western societies like Korea have come to associate Western civilization with the present and East Asian civilization with the past. Thus, within the discussions of Korean scholars, the international (or intercivilizational) cross-cultural dialogue between East and West takes on the characteristics of a cross-temporal (or diachronic) dialogue between the past and the present. Lee Seung-hwan has called for parallel cross-temporal and cross-cultural dialogues:

> The tradition to which I refer is the *quintessence* of values that have been tempered and sublimated through a harsh process of self-denial and self-verification in the midst of humiliating oppression from the outside world. It is only the dialectic of negation that can make tradition rise again in the aftermath of the devastating striking of the *old* by the *Western and the modern*. This in turn can let the resuscitated tradition strike at the modern, and can lay a majestic path that will make *tradition* truly traditional. (Lee Seung-hwan 1997, 196; emphasis original)

Biological Metaphors and the Horizon of Comparison

In order to compare diverse and divergent political theories in an effort to spatially traverse East and West and temporally traverse past and present, we may look to the biological theory of evolution, which can elucidate the mode of existence and the development of both Western and Eastern political theories. Specifically, biological concepts such as homology, analogy, and convergent/divergent evolution can provide useful insights into the nature and development of these theories.

In biology, *homology* refers to the "similarity of the structure, physiology, or development of different species of organisms"[12] stemming from a common evolutionary ancestor. *Analogy* refers to a "functional similarity of structure based not upon common evolutionary origins but upon mere similarity of use."[13] For example, the "forelimbs of such widely differing mammals as humans, bats, and deer are homologous"[14] because those mammals share a common evolutionary ancestor. The different shapes and functions of the forelimbs represent adaptive modifications that have occurred as a result of their different evolutionary processes. In contrast, the wings of birds and insects represent analogous structures. Although both types are used for flight, birds and insects do not share any common

12 Encyclopedia Britannica Online, s.v. "homology," accessed December 21, 2012, http://www.britannica.com/EBchecked/topic/270557/homology.

13 See note 12 above.

14 See note 12 above.

ancestors.

Early on, evolutionary theory stressed homology, whereas analogy was typically dismissed as a trick of nature. More recently, however, there has been renewed interest in analogy thanks to the theory of convergent evolution, which seeks to explain how species of different ancestry acquire the same or similar biological traits through their evolution in a similar ecosystem. It is interesting that *homology* relates to organisms that share a common ancestor but diverge through evolution because of different environmental needs (original affinity → divergent evolution with functional differentiation), whereas *analogy* relates to organisms with no common ancestor that converge through evolution because of similar environmental needs (original difference → convergent evolution with teleological assimilation). In this evolutionary dynamic, affinity and difference presuppose and intersect each other.

This biological knowledge can elucidate a new orientation in comparative political theory by helping us compare the theories of the East and West in terms of their vital needs (or functions) and their surrounding (natural and historical) environments–or ecosystems, if you will–without being overwhelmed by their original or current differences. To illustrate, I cite the recent theorization of Confucian constitutionalism, pioneered by Hahm Chaihark (2000). The concept of constitutionalism is widely known to have originated in the West, and liberal constitutionalism is typically associated with the rule of law, the guarantee of basic human rights, the separation of powers, judicial review, and so on. Concurrently, there is a common misbelief that the idea of constitutionalism was absent from Confucianism and other East Asian political philosophies, which are mistakenly believed to focus exclusively on arbitrary monarchical rule.

However, in tracing the origin of constitutionalism to Aristotle and Cicero in the West, we come to find that *constitution* originally referred to a "moderate and balanced form of government" or a "mixed government," rather than the full array of principles embodied by modern Western constitutionalism. According to Carl J. Friedrich (1968, 320), the idea of constitutionalism is simply a system of restraint on governmental actions, or to put it more succinctly: "How to rule the rulers?" From this perspective, constitutionalism is one of the essential problematiques that all political communities must somehow confront in order to sustain their very existence. Any political community that is not equipped with some institutional arrangement by which to check the power of rulers is surely doomed to self-destruction, for absolute power inevitably ruins rulers along with their political communities; a car with no brakes kills not only the passengers and pedestrians, but also the driver.

Following this insight, we are compelled to investigate the institutional arrangements that controlled Confucian rulers. In Confucianism, the role of checking the power of rulers relied heavily upon *li* (禮: rituals or rites), an intermediate form of doctrines existing somewhere between morals and laws. Following this path, Hahm has formulated a theory of Confucian constitutionalism, suggesting that the prime minister, royal lectures, institutionalized remonstrance, and court historians were all vital elements, in addition to the rule of *li* and its accompanying arrangements, including legal codes and customary laws (Hahm Chaihark 2000).

This kind of theorization based on the idea of convergent (analogous) or divergent (homologous) evolution transcends the facile comparison of similarities and differences between the East and West, allowing us to deepen our understanding of the original needs, spirits, and functions of a political community as well as their homologous or analogous evolution. Such a strategy would enable us to conduct a richer and more fruitful dialogue between the East and West and between the traditional and modern.

Thus, any attempt to traverse the East and West or the past and present cannot proceed from the assumption of reductive universality, which necessarily posits a particular concept, theory, or value of a given culture or civilization as universal and superior, thus suppressing the existence and value of multiplicity and difference. Instead, we must begin with the assumption of "pluralist universalism," based on a comparison between the self and the Other, and a cross-examination of their respective origins and development, which might enable us to create a "new confluent universality" (Parekh 2006, 126-27).[15] This process naturally involves self-understanding, self-criticism, and self-transcendence through constant cross-analysis of the self and the

15 Parekh (2006, 126) notes that there are three broad answers to the "question of whether there are universal moral values or norms and how we can judge other cultures . . . relativism, monism and minimum universalism." After critically examining and dismissing all three, he suggests "pluralist universalism" as an alternative, stressing the creative interplay between universal moral values and the "thick and complex moral structures of different societies, the latter domesticating and pluralizing the former and being in turn reinterpreted and revised in their light, thus leading to what I might call 'pluralist universalism'" (Parekh 2006, 127). For more of his account of the existence of universal moral values, see Parekh (2006, 127-34).

Other. Moreover, such a process would eschew the same or similar answers, which tacitly presume the inclusion of some cultures and the exclusion of others, in favor of identifying a set of primordial problematiques that every political community has been confronted and preoccupied with at some point in time and which have led to various (i.e., divergent) ideas and practices in response. At first glance, some institutions and practices seem to have originated and diverged within historically particular environments and have thus assumed apparently incommensurable forms. In reality, however, even the most distinctive political and social practices merely represent flexible responses to the fundamental needs that are shared by all political communities. In other words, the apparently diverse responses may be situated (embedded) within convergent or overlapping problematiques, comprising the values that all political communities must seek to enact, the method for enacting those values, and the way the community responds to historical vicissitudes. Returning to the ecological metaphor, such varied responses must be nurtured and respected in order to preserve biodiversity and avoiding falling into the trap of imposing a priori superiority and inferiority, in accordance with the evolutionary concepts of homology and analogy.

Conclusion

On the basis of the methodological ideas suggested in this chapter, including the concepts of transversality, cross-cultural dialogue, and analogies of convergent and divergent evolution, we can conduct comparative political theory that traverses and links seemingly contrary theories. For example, we may seek the confluence between Plato's philosopher-kings and the Confucian idea of virtuous rulers, both of which address the qualities a leader must have in order to realize an ideal state. Or we may intersect the conservatism of East Asian Confucian scholars with that of European conservatives, as both groups, despite living under radically different historical conditions, vehemently opposed the advent of liberal and industrial civilization. We may also compare the differing conceptions of public opinion as found in the principles of political legitimation given by Confucianism and liberalism or between political theories of realism, such as those of the Chinese Legalists and the Machiavellians. Likewise, we may contrast the embryonic Confucian feminism of East Asia with the early liberal feminism represented by Mary Wollstonecraft.

The exploration of such topics would represent a transversal comparison of East Asia and the West. The responses would uncover certain similarities, some of which might be attributed to a common origin and others of which would specify the fundamental needs or functions of political communities. In other words, transversal analysis can help us identify the convergent or divergent evolutionary paths of the problematiques, moving us that much closer to answering some of the profound questions in political studies. What are the minimum benefits that a political community guarantees for its members? What are the basic elements of an ideal society? Where is the ultimate locus of political legitimacy? How does a political community inherit and sustain political legitimacy? How does a political community respond to revolutionary upheavals (e.g., the Industrial Revolution, the French Revolution)? By what criteria are certain members of a political community (e.g., slaves, women, immigrants) either included or excluded? How do secular and transcendental values interact in a political community?

As I have suggested, theorists who support transversality have launched numerous attacks against universalism, the prevalence of rigid dichotomies (such as affinity vs. difference), and the essentialization of culture and civilization (including Western-centrism). These are all valid points, but I hope that I have painted a different picture with my own analysis of cross-cultural dialogue, supported by the definition of *universalism* as "widely applicable" (Lummis 2002, 69), my discussion of pluralist universalism, and the biological metaphors from the theory of evolution. Namely, such criticism seems to go too far, demonstrating the exuberant, iconoclastic zeal that seems to mark every theory in its early stages. The history of political theory in both the East and West shows us that the need to refashion and transfigure old concepts, rather than outright rejecting them, is just as important as the need to develop entirely new theories. Perhaps, transversality at its best might provide the basic foundation for a comparative political theory, whereas cross-cultural dialogue can supply a concrete method. For the guiding spirit, we need to look no further than evolutionary theory, which demonstrates that people and civilizations are never in a state of stasis or immutability, but rather exist as a steadily flowing and ever-changing wave.

References

English Materials

Appiah, Kwame Anthony. 2006. *Cosmopolitanism: Ethics in a World of Strangers.* New York: W. W. Norton.

Barry, Brian. 2001. *Culture and Equality: An Egalitarian Critique of Multiculturalism.* Cambridge, MA: Harvard University Press.

Dallmayr, Fred. 1999. "Introduction: Toward a Comparative Political Theory." In *Border Crossing: Toward a Comparative Political Theory,* edited by Fred Dallmayr, 1-10. Lanham: Lexington Books.

Fairbank, John K., Edwin O. Reischauer, and Albert M. Craig. 1989. *East Asia: Tradition and Transformation.* Rev. ed. Cambridge, MA: Harvard University Press.

Friedrich, Carl J. 1968. "Constitutions and Constitutionalism." In vol. 3 of *International Encyclopedia of Social Sciences,* edited by David L. Sills, 318-26. New York: Macmillan.

Gray, John. 1995. *Enlightenment's Wake: Politics and Culture at the Close of the Modern Age*. London: Routledge.

——. 1998. "Where Pluralists and Liberals Part Company." *International Journal of Philosophical Studies* 6 (1): 17-36.

Hahm, Chaihark. 2000. "Confucian Constitutionalism." JSD diss., Harvard Law School.

Hall, Stuart. 1992. "The West and the Rest." In *Formations of Modernity,* edited by Stuart Hall and Bram Gieben, 276-331. Cambridge, MA: Polity Press.

Huntington, Samuel P. 1996. *The Clash of Civilizations: Remaking of World Order.* New York: Simon & Schuster.

Jung, Hwa Yol. 1995. "The Tao of Transversality as a Global Approach to Truth: A Metacommentary on Calvin O. Schrag." *Man and World* 28: 11-31.

——. 1999. "Postmodernity, Eurocentrism, and the Future of Political Philosophy." In *Border Crossings: Toward a Comparative Political Theory,* edited by Fred Dallmayr, 277-96. Lanham, MD: Lexington Books.

——. 2009a. "Transversality and the Philosophical Politics of Multiculturalism in the Age of Globalization." *Research in Phenomenology* 39 (3): 416-37.

——. 2009b. "Transversality and Public Philosophy in the Age of Globalization." In *Comparative Political Theory and Cross-Cultural Philosophy: Essays in Honor of Hwa Yol Jung,* edited by Jin Y. Park, 19-54. Lanham, MD: Lexington Books.

Kang, Jung In. 1999. "Confucianism and Democracy in East Asia: A Critique of Samuel P. Huntington's *Third Wave.*" *Korea Journal* 39 (3): 316-37.

——. 2000. "Some Reflections on Recent Democratization in South Korea." *Korea Journal* 40 (2): 195-224.

——. 2003. "The Rule of Law and the Rule of Virtue: On the Necessity of Their Mutual Integration." *Korea Journal* 43 (1): 233-60.

Kang, Jung In, and Kwanyong Eom. 2003. "Comparative Analysis of Eastern and Western Tyranny: Focusing on Aristotle and Mencius." *Korea Journal* 43 (4): 113-36.

Kymlicka, Will. 1989. *Liberalism, Community and Culture.* Oxford: Clarendon Press.

——. 1995. *Multicultural Citizenship: A Liberal Theory of Minority Rights.* Oxford: Clarendon Press.

Levinas, Emmanuel. 1999. *Alterity and Transcendence.* Translated by Michael B. Smith. New York: Columbia University Press.

Lummis, C. Douglas. 2002. "Political Theory: Why It Seems Universal, but Isn't Really." *Futures* 34: 63-73.

Murphey, Rhoads. 2010. *East Asia: A New History.* 5th ed. Upper Saddle River, NJ: Longman.

Parekh, Bhikhu. 1998. "Cultural Diversity and Liberal Democracy." In *Democracy, Difference and Social Justice*, edited by Gurpreet Mahajan, 202-27. Delhi: Oxford University Press.

——. 2006. *Rethinking Multiculturalism: Cultural Diversity and Political Theory.* 2nd ed. Basingstoke: Palgrave Macmillan.

——. 2008. *A New Politics of Identity: Political Principles for an Interdependent World.* Basingstoke: Palgrave Macmillan.

Taylor, Charles. 1999. "Conditions of an Unforced Consensus on Human Rights." In *The East Asian Challenge for Human Rights,* edited by Joanne R. Bauer and Daniel A. Bell, 124-44. Cambridge: Cambridge University Press.

Taylor, Peter J. 2000. "Izations of the World: Americanization, Modernization and Globalization." In *Demystifying Globalization,* edited by Colin Hay and David Marsh, 49-70. Polis, UK: University of Birmingham.

UNESCO and International Social Science Council (ISSC). 2010. *World Social Science Report: Knowledge Divides.* Paris: UNESCO Publishing.

Wallerstein, Immanuel. 1997. "Eurocentrism and Its Avatars: The Dilemmas of Social Science." *New Left Review* 226 (November/

December): 93-107.

Korean Materials

Kang, Jung In. 2004. *Seogujungsimjuuireul Neomeoseo* [Beyond the Shadow of Western-centrism]. Seoul: Acanet.

Lee, Dong-su. 2010. "Jigu Siminui Jeongcheseonggwa Hoengdanseong" [The Identity and Transversality of a Global Citizen]. *21segi Jeongchihakhoebo* [Twenty-first Century Political Science Review] 20 (3): 181-99.

Lee, Seung-hwan. 1997. "Nuga Gamhi Jeontongeul Yokdoege Haneunga?" [Who Dare to Mock Our Tradition?]. *Jeontonggwa Hyeondae* [The Traditional and the Contemporary] 1: 176-97.

Chapter 2

The Cultural Identity of East Asia in the Age of Globalization: Westcentrism and Asian Values

The process of globalization has been accelerating since the early 1990s, notably with the end of the Cold War and the accelerated information technology (IT) revolution, which has reached its peak in the construction of the Internet with the World Wide Web. Consequently, concern about the future world order has been on the rise. With regard to the future of the various civilizations in the world, three contending views have attracted popular attention. Francis Fukuyama predicts that civilizations the world over will converge on the liberal capitalism of the West (Fukuyama 1992). In contrast, Samuel P. Huntington prophesies the clash of civilizations, especially between the West and an alliance of Islamic-Confucian civilizations, a stance that obtained for him worldwide fame after the September 11 New York terrorist attack in 2001 (Huntington 1996). In opposition to this view but without stressing convergence, Harald Müller, director of the Institute of Peace and Conflict Studies in Hesse, forecasts the coexistence of civilizations with mutual accommodation and interdependence (Müller 1999).

Thus, many Western scholars predict confidently the convergence, coexistence, or clash of civilizations in the age of globalization, placing Western civilization at the center–or as the central actor. In such glib talks about the future, non-Western civilizations remain in the background. They are frequently marginalized, forgotten, or absent. For Westerners, it appears very natural to maintain their identity while promoting globalization and a global restructuring of capitalism. In contrast, for East Asians as well as other non-Western people, the task of adapting themselves to global capitalism undergoing a major restructuring seems to entail a threat to their own identity, despite the strenuous effort hitherto put into the modernization of their own countries. In short, the task of successful adaptation to the global economic order and that of maintaining cultural identity appear mutually complementary to the former but ostensibly conflictual to the latter.

I shall explore the future of East Asian civilization in this chapter, focusing on its cultural identity in the age of globalization. To do this, first, a preliminary examination of core concepts and phenomena such as "globalization," "Westcentrism,"[1] and the "rise of East Asia" will be made, for these factors have brought the issue of East Asian cultural identity to the fore since the early 1990s. Then, in order to more concretely understand the cultural identity of East Asia in light of globalization, the cultural and economic impact of globalization upon East Asia will be investigated by discussing

1 *Eurocentrism* is the word more commonly used than *Westcentrism*. However, I prefer to use the latter, as I shall discuss later.

theories regarding the cultural effect of globalization and the tripolar regionalization of global capitalism, with special focus upon ongoing subregionalization in the Great South China and the Bohai Rim regions (GSCR and BRR, respectively). Finally, on the basis of the preceding discussions, the Asian values discourse, which is more directly related to the cultural identity of East Asia, will be reviewed and some prospective suggestions for building a viable cultural identity will be made.

Preliminary Examination

Globalization seems to have a universalizing and homogenizing impact upon people the world over, as we can find in the universalization of capitalism, democracy, the automobile, television, the Internet, and so on. However, the intensification of the cross-cultural experience made possible by globalization may frequently result in awakening and strengthening of the hitherto dormant cultural identity of peoples in many parts of the world. Because it is also an uneven and asymmetrical process and its most important source is Western civilization, led by the United States, globalization has appeared as cultural imperialism and/or another Westernization that threatens the cultural identity of most non-Western civilizations and, in turn, provokes the reactive rise of their cultural identities. In this sense globalization is Janus-faced: It is not only laden with putatively universal values but also with Westcentrism. So in order to understand the awakening of the cultural identity of East Asia since the early 1990s, it seems necessary to briefly examine globalization, Westcentrism, and the rise of East Asia.

Globalization

Globalization is a confusing and controversial concept. Jan Aart Scholte identifies at least five broad definitions of *globalization* that are interrelated and overlap in some ways.[2] First, globalization is conceived in terms of internationalization and thus refers to the increase in cross-border relations between countries. Economically it stresses "large and growing flows of trade and capital investment between countries." More broadly, it points to "enlarged movements of people, messages and ideas" between countries. Second, globalization is defined as liberalization. It means a "process of removing government-imposed restrictions on movements between countries in order to create an 'open,' 'borderless' world economy." Third, globalization is equated with universalization (i.e., the "process of spreading various objects and experiences"–e.g., the Gregorian calendar, decolonization, TVs, McDonald's–to people all over the world). Fourth, globalization is seen as "'Westernization' or modernization, especially in an 'Americanized' form." This refers to the process in which "the social structures of modernity (e.g., capitalism, rationalism, industrialism, bureaucratism) are spread the world over," generally demolishing traditional cultures and local autonomy in the process. Globalization in this sense is sometimes described as an "imperialism of McDonald's, Hollywood and CNN." Fifth, globalization is understood as

2 I draw upon Jan Aart Scholte's work on globalization heavily in the following discussion.

"deterritorialization" or a "reconfiguration of geography," by which "social space is no longer wholly mapped in terms of territorial places, territorial distances and territorial borders" (Scholte 2000, 15-17). Scholte prefers the fifth definition of globalization as a "transformation of social geography marked by the growth of supraterritorial space." He stresses, however, that "globalization does not entail the end of territorial geography," but "territoriality and supraterritoriality coexist in complex interrelations" (Scholte 2000, 8).

With regard to the causes of globalization, Scholte suggests roughly four great driving forces: the spread of rationalism as a dominant knowledge framework since the Enlightenment; a certain turn in capitalist development (for example, the globalization of production and consumption); extensive technological innovations in respect to transport, communications, and data processing; and, finally, the construction of enabling regulatory frameworks such as technical and procedural standardization, liberalization of cross-border finance, investment and trade, guarantees of property rights for global capital, and the legalization of transworld organizations and activities (Scholte 2000, 89-108).

What merits special attention in connection with the subject of this chapter is the close link between informationalization and globalization, as I shall discuss later in the subregionalization of East Asia. That is, without technological innovations, globalization patently could not have taken place. Thus, some authors suggest that technological change has been the single most important driving force behind globalization (Scholte 2000, 99). The notable impetus for it has been the IT revolution, including the construction of the Internet and the World Wide Web. Of course, the end of the Cold War, the conclusion of the Uruguay Round, and the creation of the World Trade Organization have played a significant role in accelerating globalization.

Westcentrism

The challenge of globalization is now transforming non-Western societies including East Asia, just as the challenge of modernization did a century before. Countries in East Asia have been exposed to globalization ostensibly as internationalization; that is, the free flow of information, goods, services, cultures and even social problems such as pollution, AIDS, and mad cow disease. Among these, it is information that circulates around the world in the largest amount, most freely and most rapidly. The diffusion of values and cultures has also become easier, albeit less visible, taking the form of human rights and democracy as well as the free market.[3] Thus, East Asian countries have been faced with the pressures of human rights, democratization, and market-opening from the West. Such forms of globalization will be seen as universalization and liberalization by the West but as Westernization and imperialism by East Asian countries.

Small and weak nations including countries such as Taiwan, Korea, and Thailand would find it difficult from their position to become the center in the global flow of goods, services, and values. The most important source of globalization is Western civilization

3 In the reverse, yoga, meditation, Zen Buddhism, and the like are examples of diffusion from Asia into the West.

led by the United States. The United States controls the Internet, satellite communications, and other most advanced information technologies, and more than half of world news comes from American media including CNN. Thus, the United States is the most powerful source of globalization. In the process of globalization, the values and cultures of Western civilization have diffused throughout the world. Underlying this diffusion is Westcentrism, the meta-ideology.

If we look for the words *Eurocentric* and *Eurocentrism* in *The Oxford English Dictionary* (1989, Vol. 5, 442), we find slight variations: The adjective *Europocentric* is defined as "Having or regarding Europe as its centre; presupposing the supremacy of Europe and Europeans in world culture, etc.," and the noun *Europocentrism* as "the idea or practice of placing Europe at the center of one's worldview."[4] In this chapter, however, I shall use the term *Westcentrism* instead of *Eurocentrism* because I am more interested in the current state of affairs than in the historical origin and evolution of what is called Eurocentrism, and the former more explicitly includes the United States, Canada, Australia, and the like, which have inherited and developed European civilization in non-European territories.[5]

Thus, *Westcentrism* refers to the attitude that takes the worldviews, values, institutions, and practices of Western civilization as universal and supreme. If we examine various definitions given by many theorists, the concept is found to consist of the following

4 In *The Oxford English Dictionary* the words *Eurocentric* and *Eurocentrism* are found under the entries *Europocentric* and *Europocentrism*. However, the former terms are more frequently used than the latter.

5 And, of course, the United States as the world's hegemon has set the terms and agenda of global politics more powerfully than has Europe.

three general propositions. First, modern Western civilization has reached the highest stage of development in the history of humankind (Western superiority). Second, the developmental stages in Western history are universally applicable to all human histories, applying not only to the West but also to the "Rest" (Western universalism and historicism). Third, non-Western societies placed at lower stages of development in history can improve themselves only by emulating and accepting Western civilization (Westernization/modernization thesis). In short, Westcentrism boils down to the three theses: Western superiority, Western universalism, and Westernization/ modernization.[6]

Westcentrism has evolved in the following three phases in terms of hegemonic shifts. The first hegemon of Western civilization was the Netherlands, which achieved mercantilist modernity; then it was succeeded by Great Britain, which achieved industrial modernity; and, finally, in the aftermath of World War II, Great Britain formally gave way to the United States, which actually had begun to surpass the former at least at the end of World War I with the achievement of consumerist modernity (Taylor 2000, 52). Given that the power and cultural influence wielded by the hegemons in Western civilization over neighboring Western nations have not been as powerful as those wielded by past Chinese empires over China's neighbors and that the principle of equal sovereignty among European states has been honored on the whole since the Treaty of Westphalia, widespread equality among Western nations has existed; the domination of

6 See Kang Jung In (2004b, chap. 2) for more details about the concept of Westcentrism.

the world by Western civilization in the age of colonialism and imperialism was achieved not by a single powerful nation or an empire but by the concert of Western powers.

The now-bygone twentieth century deserves the name "American Century," marked by three major US political victories: World War I, World War II, and the Cold War. In the American Century, the United States dominated the world as the leader of Western civilization and the hegemon of the world. The hegemon represents the future for other countries and wields the cultural power to restructure the world in its own image. Thus, according to Peter J. Taylor, the United States has presented the world with the project of Americanization in the postwar world. It was to offer Western European countries the benefit of consumer capitalism through the Marshall Plan and to provide decolonized countries with support for modernization. As a result, major nations in Western Europe went through the rapid reconstruction of their industry and strong Americanization in the 1950s, so they caught up with the opulent consumer capitalism of America (Taylor 2000, 58-63). In contrast, the modernization of the Third World, which was initiated by Truman's Point Four Program, aimed for the realization of nineteenth-century industrial modernity–a stage reached by the Industrial Revolution in Great Britain. However, the project failed dismally without any visible evidence for general "catching up" in the developing world. Most developing countries, except for some in East Asia and Latin America, have failed to materialize industrial capitalism, not to mention consumer capitalism.

The United States has thus projected globalization unto the

world to replace modernization and to complement Americanization since the early 1970s. With the advent of the unipolar world at the end of the Cold War, globalization has become more compelling. While both modernization and globalization are interrelated processes to complement Americanization, the latter apparently smacks of pressure and threat, whereas the former has the strong flavor of promise and persuasion (Taylor 2000, 67).

The Rise of East Asia

Kim Kyeong-il points to the context in which the phrase "East Asia" introduced itself and gained wide currency in the West:

> Although the name East Asia itself was introduced due to the demise of Eurocentrism, the establishment of American hegemony, the emergence of the Third World, and the spread of cultural relativism, it is due, above all, to the dynamic economic growth shown in this area since the 1970s that the name began to gain concrete substance common to this area. (Kim Kyeong-il 1998, 32-33)

As we may recognize in Kim's statement, East Asia had been little more than a geographic concept during the few decades after World War II. However, the dynamic economic growth achieved in this region (including Japan, Hong Kong, Taiwan, South Korea, and Singapore) since the 1970s began to attract serious attention from the West. Besides, the phenomenal economic growth observed in East and Southeast Asia and the decline of ideological confrontation in the aftermath of the Cold War have also led Asians to restore Asian consciousness or identity, so that Asia has been "rediscovered" or "re-Asianized" (Funabashi 1993, 75-77). Moreover, the Asianization of Asia is "paradoxically the result of the globalization of its economy and media." As Asian nations grow out of the special relationships with their former colonial powers and integrate with the global economy, they begin to recognize neighboring countries as "trading partners, providers of investment opportunities, and competitors" (Funabashi 1993, 79).

The dynamic growth of the East Asian economy and Asia's subsequent self-discovery forecast a new change in the world politics of the twenty-first century. Kishore Mahbubani, a Singaporean politician, stresses that there will be three centers of world power (Europe, North America, and East Asia) in the twenty-first century, in contrast to two (Europe and North America) in the twentieth century (Mahbubani 1995, 100; Gamble and Payne 1996b, 247-48). Seen from this perspective, Mahbubani asserts, the two so-called world wars and the subsequent Cold War may well be interpreted primarily as European struggles or civil wars (Mahbubani 1995, 100). In the last few centuries, Western civilization has shaped world history, and the influence of East Asia has been rather negligible. Now many observers have noted that East Asia has arrived on the world stage. Its sheer economic weight will enable it to raise its own voice and strengthen its own cultural identity. Mahbubani illustrates this point by comparing East Asia's gross national product (GNP) with that of North America over time:

> As recently as 1960, Japan and East Asia together accounted for

4 percent of world GNP, while the United States, Canada, and Mexico represented 37 percent. Today both groups have about the same share of the world's GNP (some 24 percent each), but, with more than half the world's economic growth taking place in Asia in the 1990s, the economies of North America and Europe will progressively become relatively smaller (Mahbubani 1995, 100-101).

Cultural and Economic Effects of Globalization

In order to have a prospect for the cultural identity of East Asia and examine its link with so-called Asian values in the age of globalization, we need to examine various theories regarding the cultural effect of globalization and explore an overarching reason for the coincidental rise or resurgence of Islamic fundamentalism, Asian values discourse, and Christian fundamentalism in the United States against the background of globalization. If the rise of cultural identity can be interpreted as the cultural outcome of globalization, then the tripartite regionalization of global economy, as its economic consequence. Thus, the regionalization of the global economy will be addressed with special focus on the ongoing subregionalization in the GSCR and BRR, in the process of which Asian values coagulate with globalization and informationalization.

The Cultural Effect of Globalization: The Rise of Religious Fundamentalism?

As words such as *Westernization/Americanization*, *McDonaldization*,

Coca-Colonization, and *American cultural imperialism* suggest, globalization has frequently been perceived as the inevitable and irreversible process shaping the world in the image of Western civilization, led by the United States. In particular, the globalization described in the literature of economics and business refers to the inexorable and immutable globalization of capital, culture, and communications alike, accompanied by the political logic that there is simply no other alternative. However, recent literature has begun to display growing skepticism about the logic of inevitability and irreversibility so often associated with the notion of globalization and now conceives it as a field in which trends for globalization and countertrends against it struggle and conflict with each other (Hay and Marsh 2000, 4-7, 12-13).

For the understanding of the cultural effect of globalization, Robert J. Holton's succinct summary of diverse theoretical positions seems quite useful. He divides and summarizes them roughly into the following three theses: homogenization, polarization, and hybridization.[7] Their summary is presented here in brief.

The homogenization thesis is based on the understanding of globalization as the Americanization of the global society whereby the world is reshaped in accordance with the neoliberal Washington consensus. This position is commonly found in the literature on cultural imperialism, which views the world culture as Americanized.

7 These three theses have some parallel elements with my four cultural discourse strategies to overcome Westcentrism that I examined in another paper: assimilative, reverse, syncretic, and deconstructive strategies. Of course, some equivalent to the fourth strategy (that is, the deconstructive strategy) is missing in Holton's discussion. See Kang Jung In (2004a) for more details.

This position builds on a number of key arguments. One is related to the theme of predominant American ownership of key resources for the manufacture and transmission of culture, including satellite systems, IT manufacture, news agencies, the advertising industry, television program production and export, and the film industry. A second argument focuses on the United States' role in constructing a regulatory framework within culture and information industries that favors US interests. A third argument stresses the US cultural hegemony that goes beyond US control of culture and information industries and includes the very characteristics of modern social organization. For example, the McDonaldization of society refers not merely to the spectacular worldwide expansion of the American fast food industry,[8] but more generally to certain broader cultural traits in the economy, organization, and personal life, of which McDonald's is merely a manifestation. According to a study, McDonald's corporate strategy represents the values of global rationalization such as efficiency, calculability, predictability, and control over products and the labor force. It also represents the informality and lack of status hierarchy associated with self-service. Thus, those who stress this aspect of globalization warn that the cultures of countries the world over were being converged with or homogenized to the American culture (Holton 1998, 166-72).

The polarization thesis is notably represented by Benjamin Barber and Samuel P. Huntington. This position stresses that the

8 For example, by 1994 McDonald's had five thousand restaurants abroad, including in Moscow and Beijing. By 1995, around 20 million customers were served daily around the world, and 45% of company profits derived from international operations (Holton 1998, 167-68).

dynamics of the contemporary world are far from dominated by a single logic. For Barber, "the polarization . . . is between McWorld and Jihad, between the forces of global consumer capitalism and those of retribalization, . . . between commercial artifice, technology, and pop culture on the one hand, and narrow self-righteous faiths that generate war and bloodshed on the other" (Holton 1998, 172; Barber 1996). As is mentioned in the beginning of the chapter, for Huntington, the polarization is between civilizations in general and between the West and an emergent Islamic-Confucian axis in particular. The clash of civilizations is due to economic interests and power struggles as well as cultural differences. The scenario that the clash generates is one of global civilizational war (Holton 1998, 172-73; Huntington 1996).

Finally, the hybridization thesis emphasizes "cultural hybridity," "creolization," or "syncretism" within global culture. In a variety of ways, this approach emphasizes cross-cultural borrowings and intercultural fusion and blending to create hybridized or mixed cultural forms. Much of the contemporary evidence in favor of creolization or hybridization is drawn from the sphere of music (Holton 1998, 178-84). The thesis also stresses the fluidity, indeterminacy, and openness of cross-cultural interactions, having the advantage of avoiding the burden of Westcentrism in discussing the cultural effect of globalization. Advocates of this thesis also understand the diffusion of world religions and the formation of modern European civilization as the outcome of hybridization (Nederveen Pieterse 2000, 306-7).

As the cultural identity of non-Western civilizations has been articulated in the process to challenge Westcentrism, it has more to do with bipolarization than the homogenization thesis. With regard to this, some observers have noticed the almost simultaneous rise or resurgence of Islamic fundamentalism, Asian values discourse, and Christian fundamentalism in the United States in the midst of globalization since the early 1970s.[9] Here, all three share some attributes of religious fundamentalism.[10]

Noting this trend, Arif Dirlik views the Asian values discourse as the reemergence of nationality brought about by globalization, and the resurrection of Confucianism as the outcome of economic success of East Asia and the subsequent expression of long-endured discontent with Westcentrism, which has suppressed the East Asian tradition (Dirlik 2000, 91-93). Dirlik's view has something to do with the concept of "glocalization," which was advocated and then widely circulated by Roland Robertson. Just as modern nation-states are ultimately the product of the modern international process, Asian values or East Asian discourse might well be interpreted as the outcome of regionalization or localization accompanying globalization (Nederveen Pieterse 2000, 301).

Manuel Castells suggests an overarching explanation about the coincidental rise of these religious fundamentalisms by arguing that religious fundamentalism is the most important source of constructing identity in the network society. He finds the coincidence of the birth of the IT revolution in the 1970s with the beginning of global capitalist restructuring and the beginning of the period of Islamic

9 Sometimes Hinduism is added to the list.

10 However, Confucianism as Asian values is secular, pragmatic, rational, and this-world-oriented, so the theocratic and radical attributes that characterize the other two kinds of religious fundamentalism are absent from it.

revival and purification in the Islamic world (Castells 1997, 13-14). Seen from this perspective, fundamentalist believers of Christianity, Islam, and Confucianism may well be interpreted as participants in movements to recover and maintain their collective identities, which have been threatened by globalization and informationalization, so that their response to them has appeared conservative and reactionary.

An interesting contrast here is that whereas Islamic fundamentalism in the Arab world rose in reaction to failed modernization, either in the right-wing or left-wing version, the Asian values discourse emerged later as a response to the success of capitalist industrialization. Thus, just as there exists a strong possibility that Islamic fundamentalism will be strengthened if the Islamic countries further fail in the task of modernization, so there exists a high probability that the discourse of Asian values will be dampened as the economies of East Asian countries stagnate or deteriorate, as we actually observed in the financial crises of East Asian countries in late 1990s. Such contrast may in part be related to the different orientation of the two: Islamic fundamentalism is more tied to transcendental values regardless of secular success and Asian values are more oriented to the secular success of this world.

Whereas Islamic fundamentalism and Asian values are characterized by strong anti-Westcentrism, the Christian fundamentalism existing in the United States during the Cold War era retained the attributes of anti-Communism, Westcentrism, and racism. However, the Christian fundamentalism that has resurged in America in the post-Cold War era has replaced anti-Communism with technophobia to IT–technology as a Satanic force–and hostility to the control of the United States by a world government, which the United Nations, the International Monetary Fund, and the World Trade Organization have most notably enacted and all the more so with the spur of globalization. To Christian fundamentalists, the emergence of such a new global order appears to be a threatening new uncertainty over the control of America's destiny (Castells 1997, 25-26).

Economic Effect of Globalization: Regionalization of Global Economy

As globalization becomes more pronounced with the collapse of the socialist regimes, the global economy seems to go through rapid regionalization with the formation of tripolar regional economies: the European Union, North America, and East Asia (Gamble and Payne 1996b, 251). The notably successful formation of the European Union has in turn spurred the movement toward regionalization in other areas, for it exerts increased pressure on other regions to seek regionalization to maintain their economic competitiveness. Various factors have worked in the shift of the United States toward the formation of the North American Free Trade Agreement (NAFTA). The increasing US perception of the country's declining ability to act as a global hegemon has played an important role. Thus, the increasing conflict with Japan over its "unfair" trade and the uncertainty about the future intention of the European Union, combined with sober awareness of the importance of the regional market to the US economy, led the United States to create the NAFTA (Gamble and Payne 1996b, 254-57).

In East Asia two regionalist projects are competing: the East Asia Economic Caucus (EAEC) and the Asia Pacific Economic Cooperation (APEC; Gamble and Payne 1996a; Sum 1996). In comparison with these two regionalist projects, however, most observers agree that the regionalist project in East Asia is the least well defined and the least advanced. Geographically and ideologically, East Asia shows a complex composition: Japan as an advanced economy, newly industrialized economies (South Korea, Taiwan, Hong Kong, and Singapore), the Association of Southeast Asian Nations (ASEAN), and (post-)socialist regimes comprising China, North Korea, and the countries of Indochina. Besides, there is no single center that could shape a regionalist project into a coherent form with vigor. The willingness or the capacity of the two potential regional hegemons—that is, Japan and China—to take the leadership is still uncertain or dubious. Besides, two other great powers, the United States and Russia, are involved in the region.

In regard to the subject of this chapter, thus, the subregionalization of the East Asian economy in GSCR and the BRR merits special attention. These cases show clearly how globalization, informationalization, and cultural homogeneity are interwoven into shaping a subregional economic integration without creating any formal institutional mechanisms, bypassing the thorny issue of the sovereignty of the states involved. To be more specific about the role these factors play, globalization dictates the need for mutually beneficial economic division of labor in the area to meet the challenge of restructuring the capitalism of the countries involved. Cultural homogeneity, which is absent from the APEC and the EAEC, is provided by ethnic ties and Asian values. Informationalization facilitates the economic integration and the cohesiveness of Asian values. The cases also show that Asian values are effective not only in promoting economic development at the state level, but also in forging synergic economic integration beyond it.

To illustrate this point, a brief summary of Cho Myung-Rae's excellent research on what he calls "transborder network capitalism" in the GSCR and the BRR seems mandatory, without going into technical details of the political economy at the same time. According to Cho, these two regions are governed and integrated increasingly by transborder networks and geogovernance. By *transborder networks*, Cho refers to "the economic networks which extend and function across the different national systems of production, trade and finance, each system at work within the regulatory bound of a sovereign economy." By *geogovernance*, he means "the underlying mechanisms which govern the transborder flows of materials, information and commodities through the networks of intra-, inter-, and extra-firm relations." According to him, "[t]he mechanisms of geogovernance include, for instance, technical and managerial integration, financial and trade regulation, ethnic and personal ties, political mediations, intergovernmental agreements, all underpinning a national governance system and its articulation with others" (Cho Myung-Rae 1997, 1).

On the basis of these key concepts, Cho examines the formation of transborder network capitalism in the two regions. First, the network capitalism in the GSCR that incorporates China's Guandong, Fujian, and Jiansu provinces, Hong Kong, and Taiwan is composed of the tripartite combination of Taiwanese capital and manufacturing technology, Chinese cheap labor and materials, and Hong Kong's financial and trading mediation as the economic division of labor. Here, the major actors in the joint ventures are the small and medium-sized firms from Taiwan and Hong Kong, the local/provincial Chinese governments, and quasi-public enterprises (Cho Myung-Rae 1997, 5-7).[11] The main mechanisms of geogovernance in the region are the market and local community (Cho Myung-Rae 1997, 10-11). And according to Cho, these are complemented by two subsidiary mechanisms, Asian values and informationalization, in the following way:

> One is cultural, ethnic and linguistic commonalities which are embedded in interpersonal ties, family life, community practices and the sense of territory. . . . In the Chinese business system, their traditional relational mechanism called *guanxi* makes up for a lack in the rule of law, and transparency in rules and regulation. . . . The other is telecommunication infrastructures which give support to the trans-spatial and -temporal coordination through the cyberspace. The GSCR is famous worldwide for the good or rapidly improving infrastructural systems which include wider trunk-road connections, high-tech-based telecommunication networks, excellent hub ports (teleports, airports, seaports) and the like. . . . Both mechanisms are combined to create [an] ethnic-spatial bond which works as

11 However, given that Hong Kong was returned to China in 1997, the original tripartite relationship was transformed (although not much changed functionally) into a bilateral relationship between Taiwan and the southern Chinese provinces including Hong Kong, Guangdong, and Fujian (Cho Myung-Rae 1997, 5).

> the force of meta-geogovernance over the space of the GSCR. (Cho Myung-Rae 1997, 11)

In contrast, the transborder network capitalism in the BRR incorporates China's three northeastern provinces (Shandong, Laioning, Hebei) and two provincial-level cities there (Beijing and Tianjin) and the central west coastal region (especially, Kyunggi province) of Korea. The transnational space in the region has been constructed since the early 1990s, especially after the historic Korea-China diplomatic normalization in 1992. The construction was initiated primarily by Korean large companies (*chaebol*) on the one hand, and the Chinese central government and state-owned firms on the other, with the former's contribution of capital and technologies and the latter's provision of a market (Cho Myung-Rae 1997, 12).

Korean firms prefer the northeastern provinces "primarily for geographical proximity (about 100 sea miles) and cultural and ethnic affinity, as well as for its regional production conditions complementary to Korea's new globalizing economy" (Cho Myung-Rae 1997, 12). Korean companies there build networks with Chinese partners to secure a hierarchical and integrative management system favorable to market control, as they have done in Korea. The two main mechanisms for geogovernance in the region are hierarchy and the state (Cho Myung-Rae 1997, 17-18).[12] There are two further

12 According to Cho Myung-Rae, *hierarchy mechanism* refers to an "organizational principle which enforces the vertical integration of all associated business activities, thereby internalizing arm's-length transactions within the centralized ownership structure," and *state mechanism* to "political arrangements at a state level to govern and balance diverse and sometimes conflicting institutions,

mechanisms to complement them for their effective functioning in the BRR, which play a role similar to what we find in the GSCR: "Korean ethnic community and the cyberspace of Korean multinationals." For Koreans, the Northeastern provinces of China constitute what Benedict Anderson has called an "imagined community" due to the presence of two million ethnic Korean residents there. Thus, just as overseas Chinese prefer to invest in South China by taking advantage of their community networks, so do Koreans in the northeastern provinces (Cho Myung-Rae 1997, 18). According to Cho, "[t]his imaginary spatial identity activates a strong geo-cultural mechanism to foster the cross-border interaction between Korea and China" (Cho Myung-Rae 1997, 18). In addition, the cyberspace built through the electronic communication networks that link the Korean headquarters with local plants in China consolidate the governance mechanism that maintains and coordinates transborder flows (Cho Myung-Rae 1997, 18). According to Cho, thus the GSCR and the BRR, which have been incorporated into the cyberspace, are no longer the exclusive domain of a sovereign state, but the "virtual space for multiple encounters among contending actors–small and large firms, Korean and Chinese, local and global players"–that also transmits and consolidates Asian values in terms of personal ties and business culture (Cho Myung-Rae 1997, 18-19).

Cho's study shows how global capitalism works out glocalization at the supranational level (beyond the state) by taking advantage of the universal mechanism of information technologies and combining

organizations, firms, and workers involved in the transnational operations of Korean firms" (Cho Myung-Rae 1997, 17-18).

them with cohesive Asian values, the particular business culture and human relationships unique to the region. Thus Cho predicts that the possibility for the emergence of East Asia as an economic bloc in tripartite global capitalism depends upon the formation of network capitalism, which articulates and shares a similar mode of development and cultural identity through the interactive learning process of regional actors (Cho Myung-Rae 1997, 23).

Asian Values and the Cultural Identity of East Asia

The Asian values (or East Asian) discourse has risen more vocally in East Asia since the early 1990s, in reaction to the American version of Westcentrism represented by modernization and globalization. From this perspective, Kim Kwang-eok interprets "East Asian discourse" as a "reactive product of critical reflection upon modernization theory based on the Western discourse"–a reflexive attempt to find explanation for the phenomenal economic growth in East Asia by East Asians who used to believe that development is impossible without resorting to what is Western–and/or as the discourse resulting from the desire and confidence of East Asian societies that seek to form a defensive community to counter the diffusion of a Westcentric world system (Kim Kwang-eok 1998, 5-6). In a similar vein, Kim Gi-bong defines it as the "response to the challenge of globalization, another name of imperialism" (Kim Gi-bong 2001, 13).

With this context in mind, let us examine the Asian values discourse more closely.[13] According to Jeon Je-guk's succinct summary, the Asian values discourse refers to the argument that the communitarianism based on Confucian culture is much superior to Western individualism in creating and maintaining an orderly and healthy society.[14] Thus, the advocates of Asian values criticize Western civilization, notably the United States, for its retrogressive phenomena rooted in individualism—for example, extreme individualism, selfishness, lack of discipline and self-indulgence, the dissolution of family and the rapid increase in unwed motherhood and juvenile delinquency, rampant increase in drug use, violence, and crimes, inferior education, and the breakdown of civil society. In contrast, they assert that the relative superiority of Asian values enables Asians to maintain an orderly and healthy society. For them, the superiority of Asian values consists of familism, filial piety, and loyalty, the communitarianism that stresses the community and social order over individual members, respect for authority, stress on social order and discipline over individual freedom, preference for consensus and harmony over competition and confrontation, thrifty and diligent lifestyle, and so on (Jeon Je-guk 1999, 195-96).

The rise of the Asian values discourse requires the understanding of its political dimension as well as the economic one. Although

13 See Kim Kwang-eok (1998), Suhl Han (2000), and Kim Gi-bong (2001) for Korean scholars' critical review of the Asian values discourse.

14 Although Asian values are commonly associated with Confucianism, they are not necessarily so, as political leaders of Malaysia whose predominant religion is Islam assert them as well. But in this chapter I associate Asian values primarily with Confucianism, following common practice.

the origin of globalization could be traced back to the period before the 1990s, the breakdown of the socialist regimes and their subsequent liberalization in the 1990s appeared to vigorously fuel the globalization of triumphant capitalism and liberal democracy all over the world. Consequently, the US offensive toward East Asian countries has been launched on a full scale, demanding respect for human rights and "fair" trade. In order to check the rise of Asian powers, the United States began to accuse authoritarian regimes in the region of violating human rights and called for the abolition of "unfair" trade barriers and practices hitherto excused. Seen from this perspective, the most significant events triggering the Asian values discourse are, above all, the phenomenal economic growth of East Asian countries in contrast to economic stagnation in the West and the abrupt demise of socialist regimes, as well as the quarrels between the United States and East Asian countries surrounding human rights issues.

In order to counter this American offensive, some political leaders of Asian countries rejected the superiority and universality of Western values–that is, the main assumptions of Westcentrism–and, instead, asserted the superiority and universality of Asian values. In particular, the Singaporean government and the so-called Singaporean school, including Lee Kwan Yew, raised the Asian values discourse more vigorously, on the basis of newly attained pride coming from the economic success of East Asian countries, as an effective slogan to counter Western pressures (Fukuyama 1998, 258).[15] Here the human

15 With regard to the background of the emergence of Asian values discourse in Singapore, see Kim Myeong-su (2000). Kim stresses domestic factors–that is, attempts to solve the identity crisis of Chinese residents there through some

rights issue came to the fore as a focal issue between the West and East Asia in the aftermath of the Cold War. Subsequently, China joined in the Asian values discourse. Confronted with the US-initiated Western criticism of human rights violations in China, the Chinese government previously defended its position with the conventional socialist critique of human rights as bourgeois ideology, but it has now shifted to defend it in terms of Chinese cultural tradition (Moody 1996, 175-82). Thus in 1993, a caucus of Asian countries meeting in Bangkok prior to a major international human rights conference in Geneva proclaimed that "human rights are, in practice, contingent upon culture, history, the level of economic development and the like, and that the West has no business imposing its views on others" (Moody 1996, 166). In this way, the Asian values have been (ab)used actively by governments in Asia to defend themselves against Western criticism of their human rights violations and authoritarianism.

In addition, it should be noted that the Asian values discourse also contains the fear that Asian society would be plagued with Western pathological diseases as a consequence of the diffusion of Western values into Asian societies, which has been made possible by economic development and subsequently accelerated by globalization and informationalization. If left unattended, Asian societies would fall into the decay and degeneracy of the contemporary American scene (Jeon Je-guk 1999, 166; Moody 1996, 188-92). As a matter of fact, many observers–including even Lee Kwan Yew–predict that so-called Asian values will recede as rapid economic development enables Asian

cultural prescriptions–over external factors in his explanation of the emergence of the Asian values discourse in Singapore.

countries to reach an affluent consumer society and globalization and informationalization proceed further in the future (Kim Myeong-su 2000). In this regard, Dirlik also argues that the resurgence of Confucianism is in part a response provoked by the intrusion of a global consumer culture (Dirlik 2000, 103).

In order to find the link between the Asian values discourse and Asian cultural identity in a more concrete way, an examination of the Asian values discourse in light of the three theses with regard to the cultural effect of globalization seems necessary.

First, the Asian values discourse does not appear to accord well with the homogenization thesis and rather confirms the bipolarization thesis, as it stresses the difference between Asian and Western values and the former's superiority over the latter. However, if the discourse suggests Asian values as the functional equivalent to Weber's famous Protestant ethic in the development of capitalism, then it might be interpreted as supportive of the homogenization thesis. In this regard, Dirlik explains some American scholars' enthusiastic applause of Asian values as the attempt to universalize and legitimate Western capitalism beyond the West in the age of global capitalism, although Asian values appear opposed to Western values (Dirlik 2000, 106-7). If we take this interpretation, then, the discourse would boil down to nothing more than what Immanuel Wallerstein has called "anti-Eurocentric Eurocentrism," thereby paradoxically joining the homogenization thesis (Wallerstein 1997, 101-4). Furthermore, if we apply the concept of anti-Eurocentric Eurocentrism to Asian values' positive contribution to capitalist industrialization, then the Asian values discourse accepts the significance of capitalism as a positive value (or achievement) "in precisely the terms that Europe has defined it," although asserting that Asians can develop capitalism as well as, or far better than, Europeans by taking advantage of Asian values (Wallerstein 1997, 103).

Francis Fukuyama also supports the homogenization thesis by predicting that Asian values will weaken or disappear with the further progress of economic development and globalization (Fukuyama 1998). This corresponds to his major argument presented in *The End of History* that world history converged on liberalism and capitalism with the end of the Cold War. If we take Fukuyama's position, then, the Asian values discourse may well be interpreted as a nostalgic, reactionary discourse confessing that Asians have crossed a bridge of no return by rapid economic development and affluence. In this sense, the discourse could be interpreted as an expression of the traditional generation's discontent with the diffusion of Western values such as licentious libertinism and extreme individualism into their own society by way of modernization and globalization, rather than as their active resistance to the external Western pressures. Then it turns out to be more for domestic consumption than for external defense against Western criticism.

Second, scholars such as Huntington and Barber may interpret the Asian values discourse as indicative of the bipolarization thesis. Huntington explicitly takes the discourse as evidence that proves the validity of the bipolarization thesis, and he predicts the clash of civilizations between the Western and Confucian-Islamic civilizations in his *Clash of Civilizations*. However, in the case of Barber, it is not clear whether he thinks so with regard to the Asian values discourse, although he conceives of Islamic fundamentalism as opposed to Western civilization. Although the logic is loose, Tu Weiming seems to support the bipolarization thesis because he argues that Asian economic development suggests the model of a "third industrial civilization" as opposed to the Western capitalist model and the Soviet socialist model, adding that there exists a thick cultural foundation for it (Tu Weiming 1995, 382).

Finally, we might ask whether the Asian values discourse constitutes the hybridization thesis. In connection with this, we need to be reminded that advocates of Asian values do not repudiate democracy, human rights, and capitalism originating from the West, in a wholesale way, although they might display strong reservations about liberalism and individualism. They do not propose viable and explicit alternatives to capitalism and democracy, either. Besides, the advocates stress Asian values as favorable to capitalist industrialization, which means, after all, capitalism is the criterion against which the value of Asian values is assessed regard to human rights, they seem to deny the universal application of human rights rather than the concept of human rights in itself. Furthermore, they have not been successful in presenting a viable and coherent alternative to the Western notion of human rights. At most, they emphasize the need for some minor revision in concept and partial reservation in application.[16] All this considered, it seems difficult to interpret that they support the bipolarization thesis insofar as capitalism, human rights, and democracy are concerned. Instead, the discourse seems

16 However, the discourse usually takes a negative attitude toward Western individualism and feminism, thereby approaching the bipolarization thesis in these aspects.

to suggest that "the traditional value systems provide at least as good a foundation for modernity as do those derived from the West" (Moody 1996, 169). Then, as the hybrid concepts such as "Confucian capitalism," "Confucian democracy," and "Asian-style democracy" suggest,[17] the discourse supports the hybridization thesis and implies a hybrid cultural identity in the making.

Thus, theoretical attempts to hybridize capitalism and democracy with distinctive Asian values suggest the formation of a hybrid cultural identity in East Asia by stressing the contribution of Asian values to the development of capitalism and democracy and subsequently legitimizing capitalism and democracy of Western origin in terms of Asian values.[18] For example, with regard to capitalism, Kim Il-gon argues that "capitalism as a system, however universal it may be, cannot change particularities derived from cultural diversity and differences so completely as to make the world economic order monistic and uniform" (Kim Il-gon 1999, 48). On the basis of such an assumption we may well classify the types of capitalism in the world, for example, into the following three models: the "competitive capitalism" of the United States, the "welfare capitalism" of Western Europe, and the "Confucian symbiotic capitalism" of East Asia (Kim Il-gon 1999) or the Anglo-American "free-market model," the European "politically bargained model," and the Japanese "socially integrated model" (Cho Myung-Rae 1997, 2). If such a classification is established with validity, then room opens up for supposing diverse

17 See Neher (1994) and Kim Yung-Myung (1997) for the debate over "Asian-style democracy."

18 Remember that the legitimacy of capitalism and democracy was flatly denied by most of the traditional elites of East Asia in the nineteenth century.

models of capitalism, instead of insisting on the US or European model as universal. Then, commonalities shared by American, European, and East Asian models of capitalism (e.g., the overall recognition of private property and enterprises, the existence of free market) may be recognized as universal traits of capitalism, whereas the differences (e.g., differences in social welfare systems, the degree of state intervention, the relationship between management and labor) displayed by each model may constitute cultural identity for the people belonging to it. In this way, capitalism existing in the United States and Europe as well as that in East Asia will be conceived of as respective subcategories of universal capitalism.[19]

With regard to democracy, East Asia has not been successful in developing a distinct model. However, we are reminded that there have been diverse forms of democracies in the West, and consequently various attempts to classify them–for example, liberal versus social democracy, majoritarian versus consensual democracy, liberal versus communitarian democracy, and the presidential versus parliamentary system–have been made. Thus, as democracies in East

19 In regard to this, we may look back over monarchies in premodern ages. For example, there had universally been hereditary kingship in premodern Europe and East Asia. To make a rough comparison, there were feudal and absolute monarchies in Europe, whereas there were Confucian and Japanese-style monarchies in East Asia. There must have been significant differences among them due to economic-cultural differences as well as commonalities such as hereditary kinship. Thus it might be possible to conceive of monarchies in Europe and East Asia on an equal basis as subtypes of universal hereditary kingship without assigning hierarchical value to either of them. Following this reasoning, although capitalism and democracy originated in the West uniquely and then were adopted derivatively later in East Asia, we may well categorize them equally as viable subtypes, as they develop in East Asia in a full-fledged form.

Asia evolve into more mature ones, they may well develop a "third subtype" of democracy that is distinct from Western models, or close to some form of communitarian democracy, given that East Asian countries have a strong communal culture in contrast to the Western individualist culture. In this vein, Daniel Bell, a professor now at Tsinghua University, once conceptualized democracies in East Asia as a type of communitarian democracy, calling it "illiberal democracy" (Bell 1995). However, some Western scholars characterized nascent democracies in East Asia in the 1990s as "Asian-style democracy" (Neher 1994) or "dominant party democracy' (Huntington 1991), both of which appear to characterize democracies in Asia as deviant from normal and normative Western democracies. This conceptualization, however, seemed to be too cursory at best and too arrogant at worst, considering Asians' as yet short-term experiments with democracy.[20]

In order to avoid such cursory theorization, it might be useful to note the Chinese accommodation of Buddhism in the past. In the first century or so, Buddhism was transmitted from India to China, and, consequently, China became Buddhist. However, as the Confucian and Taoist tradition remained strong and the Chinese adapted Buddhism to their purposes and needs, the indigenization of Buddhism went on, ultimately giving birth to the distinctive Chinese-style Buddhism that would become the standard model for further variations in Korea and Japan. In a similar way, East Asian countries have experienced modernization–notably, the formation of nation-states, capitalist industrialization, and democratization–belatedly

20 See Kang Jung In (1999, 2000) for a critique of such theoretical trends.

and most intensely among non-Western civilizations in the last one hundred fifty years. At an early phase the Westernization of East Asia proceeded eagerly and, to a certain extent, inevitably. At a later phase with the success of initial Westernization, the indigenization of Western institutions and values–the Asianization of Western modernity, capitalism, and democracy–is bound to take place, either consciously or unconsciously. The rise of Asian values discourse is clear evidence supporting it. It will take more time for this process to give birth to distinctive varieties of capitalism and democracy in East Asia in the end. In that process, it will be found with the benefit of hindsight that universal and particular elements of Western capitalism and democracy are to be separated from each other; the former are to remain universal as before, while the latter are to be replaced by elements particular to East Asian varieties, so that hybrid forms may appear as another alternative type to the Western models. Seen from this perspective, we might say, contemporary East Asian civilization is in the making as a kind of hybrid, going through the dialectical process of "Westernization" of Asian civilization and "Asianization" of Western civilization.[21]

Conclusion

As the preceding examination suggests, it is difficult to develop a coherent position with regard to the effects of globalization upon

21 Masakazu Yamazaki (1996) and Kishore Mahbubani (1995) develop reasoning similar to this.

the cultural identity of East Asia, as they vary with the area of examination, developmental stage, level of abstraction, and theorists' worldview.[22] For example, we may find homogenization in sports, bipolarization in religion, and hybridization in food and music. Initially homogenization may be predominant, later bipolarization, and finally hybridization.

If we evaluate the three theses at the abstract level, whereas the homogenization and bipolarization theses in their explanation of the cultural effect of globalization are so simplistic as to be falsified with ease, the hybridization thesis has difficulty in clarifying and specifying the terms of hybridization (i.e., unevenness, asymmetry, and inequality existing in combination) of Western and other civilizations (e.g., East Asian, Hindu, Islamic, Latin American, African civilizations), so it is open to the criticism that it is confusing and elusive and at best a post hoc explanation. However, considering the long duration of cultural evolution, on the whole the hybridization thesis seems more reasonable and persuasive. Besides, the hybridization thesis has a progressive aspect, as it denies the essentialist assumption that civilization is fixed and unchangeable.

However, the three theses are not necessarily exclusive functionally and logically. For example, in the clashing and converging process of diverse cultures and civilizations made possible by globalization, the homogenization thesis confirms the universal elements, while the bipolarization thesis recognizes the unique elements that secure each civilization its cultural identity. Then

22 This is all the more so as globalization is not a completed but an ongoing process.

the hybridization thesis articulates or sums up the final synthesis of emulative homogenization and identity-forming differentiation (bipolarization). This insight suggests that the exploration of the cultural identity of East Asian civilization in a more systematic and concrete way requires further research on the theoretical and empirical aspects of the hybridization thesis.

References

English Materials

Barber, Benjamin. 1996. *Jihad vs. McWorld: How Globalism and Tribalism Are Reshaping the World.* New York: Ballantine.

Bell, Daniel. 1995. "Democracy in Confucian Societies: The Challenge of Justification." In Daniel Bell et al., *Towards Illiberal Democracy in Pacific Asia*, 17-40. New York: St. Martin's Press.

Castells, Manuel. 1997. *The Power of Identity*. Oxford: Blackwell Publishers.

Cho, Myung-Rae. 1997. "Transborder Networks and Geogovernance: A Comparison of the Great South China Region and the Bohai Rim Region," 1-28. Paper presented at the International Conference of Regional Studies Association held in Frankfurt, Germany, Sept. 20-23, 1997.

Fukuyama, Francis. 1992. *The End of History and the Last Man*. New York: Free Press.

Funabashi, Yoich. 1993. "The Asianization of Asia." *Foreign Affairs* 72:5 (September/October): 75-85.

Gamble, Andrew, and Anthony Payne, eds. 1996a. *Regionalism and World Order*. London: Macmillan.

——. 1996b. "Conclusion: The New Regionalism." In Andrew Gamble and Anthony Payne, 247-64.

Hay, Colin, and David Marsh. 2000. "Introduction: Demystifying Globalization." In *Demystifying Globalization*, edited by Colin Hay and David Marsh, 1-17. Polis, UK: University of

Birmingham.

Holton, Robert J. 1998. *Globalization and the Nation-State*. London: Macmillan.

Huntington, Samuel P. 1991. *The Third Wave*. Norman: University of Oklahoma Press.

——. 1996. *The Clash of Civilizations and the Remaking of World Order*. New York: Simon & Schuster.

Kang, Jung In. 1999. "Confucianism and Democracy in East Asia: A Critique of Samuel P. Huntington's *Third Wave*." *Korea Journal* 39 (3): 316-37.

——. 2000. "Some Reflections on Recent Democratization in South Korea." *Korea Journal* 40 (2): 195-224.

——. 2004a. "Beyond Eurocentrism: Reexamining Cultural Discourse Strategies to Overcome Eurocentrism in the Context of Polycentric Multiculturalism." *The Korean Political Science Review* 38 (4): 183-200.

Kim, Yung-Myung. 1997. "'Asian-Style Democracy': A Critique from East Asia." *Asian Survey* 37 (12): 1119-34.

Mahbubani, Kishore. 1995. "The Pacific Way." *Foreign Affairs* 74 (1): 100-111.

Moody, Peter R., Jr. 1996. "Asian Values." *Journal of International Affairs* 50 (1): 166-92.

Neher, Clark D. 1994. "Asian Style Democracy." *Asian Survey* 34 (11): 949-61.

The Oxford English Dictionary. 1989. "Europocentrism." In vol. 5. Oxford: Clarendon.

Scholte, Jan Aart. 2000. *Globalization: A Critical Introduction*. New York: St. Martin's Press.

Sum, Ngai-Ling. 1996. "The NICs and Competing Strategies of East Asian Regionalism." In Andrew Gamble and Anthony Payne, 207-45.

Taylor, Peter J. 2000. "Izations of the World: Americanization, Modernization and Globalization." In *Demystifying Globalization*, edited by Colin Hay and David Marsh, 49-70. Polis, UK: University of Birmingham.

Wallerstein, Immanuel. 1997. "Eurocentrism and Its Avatars: The Dilemmas of Social Science." *New Left Review* 226 (November/December): 93-107.

Yamazaki, Masakazu. 1996. "Asia, a Civilization in the Making." *Foreign Affairs* 75 (4): 106-18.

Korean Materials

Dirlik, Arif. 2000. "Yeoksawa Daeripdoeneun Munhwainga? Dongasia Jeongcheseongui Jeongchihak." [Culture against History: The Politics of East Asian Identity]. In *Balgyeoneuroseoui Dongasia* [East Asia as a Discovery], edited by Mun-gil Chung, Won-sik Choi, Young-seo Paik, and Hyoung-jun Cheon, 80-112. Seoul: Munhakgwajiseongsa. Originally presented at an international conference ("Searching for an East Asian Identity"), Seoul, September 30-October 1, 1999.

Fukuyama, Francis. 1998. "Wigi Ihu Asiajeok Gachi Sarajinda" [Asian Values Will Disappear after the Crisis]. *Shindonga* [New East Asia] (May): 256-63.

Jeon, Je-guk. 1999. "'Asiajeok Gachi' Gwallyeon Dongseononjaengui Jaejomyeong" [The East-West Debates over "Asian Values" Reexamined]. *Hangukgwa Gukjejeongchi* [Korea and World Politics] 15 (1): 187-219.

Kang, Jung In. 2004b. *Seogujungsimjuuireul Neomeoseo* [Beyond the Shadow of Westcentrism]. Seoul: Acanet.

Kim, Gi-bong. 2001. "Dongasia Damnon, Eodiseo Wasseumyeo Eodiro Gaya Haneunga: Jegukjuuirobuteo Jegukjuuireul Neomeoseo" [Whither the East Asian Discourse? From Imperialism to Beyond Imperialism]. *Dongasia Munhwawa Sasang* [Culture and Thought of East Asia] 6: 12-38.

Kim, Il-gon. 1999. "Yugyojeok Jabonjuuiui Inganjonjunggwa Gongsaengjuui" [Respect for Human Dignity and the Principle of Symbiosis in Confucian Capitalism]. *Dongasia Munhwawa Sasang* [Culture and Thought of East Asia] 2: 28-60.

Kim, Kwang-eok. 1998. "Dongasia Damnonui Munhwajeok Uimi" [Cultural Meaning of the East Asian Discourse]. *Jeongsinmunhwayeongu* [Spiritual Culture Studies] 21 (1): 3-25.

Kim, Kyeong-il. 1998. "Dongasiawa Segyechejeiron" [East Asia and the World-System Theory]. *Jeongsinmunhwayeongu* [Spiritual Culture Studies] 21 (1): 27-45.

Kim, Myeong-su. 2000. "Asiajeok Gachiui Munhwajeok Giwon: Singgaporeu Junghwaminjogui Jeongcheseong Wigi" [The Cultural Origin of Asian Values: The Identity Crisis of Chinese Residents in Singapore]. *Jeontonggwa Hyundae* [The Traditional and the Contemporary] (Spring): 268-89.

Müller, Harald. 1999. *Munmyeongui Gongjon* [The Coexistence of Civilizations]. Translated by Young-hui Lee. Seoul: Pureunsup. Originally published as *Zusammenleben der Kulturen: ein Gegenentwurf zu Huntington* (Frankfurt am Main: Fischer Taschenbuch Verlag GmbH, 1998).

Nederveen Pieterse, Jan. 2000. "Honyunghwaroseoui Segyehwa"

[Globalization as Hybridization]. In *Keundaisong, Talkeurtdaisong gurigo Sekyehwa* [Modernity, Postmodernity, and Globalization], edited and translated by Min-jae Yoon, 294-324. Seoul: Sahoemunhwa Yeonguso. Originally published as "Globalization as Hybridization," in *Global Modernities*, edited by Mike Featherstone, Scott Lash, and Roland Robertson, 45-68 (London: Sage, 1995).

Suhl, Han. 2000. "'Asiajeok Gachi' Nonjaeng: Bopyeonseonggwa Teuksuseong" [The Debates over "Asian Values": Their Universality and Particularity]. *Dongbugayeongu* [Journal of Northeast Asian Studies] 5: 299-329.

Tu, Weiming. 1995. "Uga Cheolhakgwa Hyeondaehwa" [Confucian Philosophy and Modernization]." In Dongasia, Munje wa Sigak, [East Asia: Problems and Perspectives], edited by Mun-kil Chung, Won-sik Choi, Young-seo Paik and Hyeong-jun Jeon, 333-90. Seoul: Munhakkwa Jisongsa.

Chapter 3

The Rule of Law and the Rule of Virtue: On the Necessity of Their Mutual Integration

Since its independence, South Korea has introduced and accommodated Western political institutions and ideas, including the rule of law, and has proclaimed itself in its constitution to be a democratic republic. However, for a variety of reasons, the rule of law has not been fully consolidated, so its legal order has remained in a state of considerable disorder.

Korean society is suffering from a paradox–the simultaneous excess and dearth of the rule of law. While a great number of laws regulating politicians and citizens are produced daily, they do not have much effect on society. The ruling elite of successive governments has not hesitated to violate laws in order to maintain power. Although a bill of rights is clearly stated in Korea's constitution, respect for human rights still remains low among public officials. Common citizens also do not hesitate to violate the law for their private gain and convenience even now, three decades after the beginning of the democratic transition in 1987.[1]

The situation in Western societies does not seem much different. Despite an elaborate legal system and strict law enforcement, crime and deviant behaviors are increasing all the more. In addition, cases in which violators of the law escape convictions by employing highly paid and highly competent lawyers are common in the United States. Thus, a Korean saying–"Guilty if you don't have money, innocent if you have money"–seems to apply to the United States as well.

The so-called prisoner's dilemma–an exemplary case in game theory–also dramatizes a situation in which criminals who commit the same crime together are preoccupied with finding a "rational" strategy to minimize their punishment, while weighing and calculating the potential effects of confession. An enthusiastic engagement with such game theory is a testimony to the sick and gloomy reality that the conscience of good citizens–and the belief that one should willingly confess to a crime with moral repentance–is completely lost. In fact, the theory academically reproduces and legitimizes unabashedly the actual flaws of the rule of law.

The solution to such problems facing the contemporary Rechtsstaat (constitutional state) should be either to further strengthen the rule of law or to search for alternatives. Here we are reminded of the benign influence of the rule of virtue, which operated as the ruling principle in traditional Confucian culture. For even if the legal system were elaborated to the fullest degree, it would only remain so on paper without contributing to the moral improvement

1 Of course, it cannot be denied that there has been considerable progress in adapting the rule of law and respect for human rights since 1987.

of public officials and citizens. The idea of the rule of virtue originated from the sober awareness of such problems inherent in the rule of law and aimed for the direct moral improvement of citizens. The rule of law, which demands external obedience to the law, and the rule of virtue, which stresses inward adherence to moral norms, are principles that not only do not conflict, they reinforce and complement each other. Thus, the academic comparison of these principles in terms of their strengths and limitations has significant practical implications for integrating them into an intertwined whole.

The purpose of this chapter, then, is to present an argument that the rule of virtue is necessary to complement the rule of law in contemporary democracies; this will be accomplished by examining the overall development of the rule of law in contrast to the rule of virtue in the history of both Western and East Asian political thought. For this purpose, in the second section I summarize the views of modern Western thinkers who asserted that the rule of law was absent in the non-Western world and briefly define the key concepts used in this chapter, such as the *rule of virtue*, the *rule of* li,[2] the *rule of law*, and *constitutionalism*. In the third and fourth sections I examine the development of the idea of the rule of law (given that it is the dominant of the two principles in the contemporary world), focusing on major ancient political theorists of the West and East Asia, while at the same time showing that all civilized societies have actually pursued the integration of the two systems. Thus, in the third section, I examine the development of the idea of the rule of

2 *Li* (禮) is commonly translated as "rite(s)" or "ritual(s)." Sometimes *li* is translated as "propriety" in this chapter, for *li* stipulates or regulates proper speech and behavior.

law, primarily focusing on Plato, Aristotle, and Cicero, and then try to show that the idea of the rule of virtue was integrated with the idea of the rule of law in their legal philosophy. In the fourth section, I examine the conventional status of the rule of law in the history of Chinese political thought with special focus on the pre-Qin era, examine the integration of the two principles in the political thought of Confucius and Mencius, and discuss the Confucian idea of the rule of *li* in comparison with the Western idea of constitutionalism. In the concluding section, I argue that respect for the law, which is indispensable to the modern ideal of the rule of law, is actually the outcome of the rule of virtue, thereby stressing that the modern rule of law should be complemented by the rule of virtue.

Preliminary Examination

The Orient Lacking the Rule of Law

Modern Western intellectuals actively engaged in translating Western military and economic dominance into cultural and intellectual superiority in the process of Western expansion into and conquest of many parts of the globe. Underlying such a task was the Eurocentric *weltanschauung* (worldview). Eurocentrism was typically formulated using simplistic dichotomies, and the typical logic was to point out that "something does not exist in the 'Rest,' though it does in the West." If we take capitalism as an example, the typical question that Western intellectuals usually posed was "Why did capitalism develop in the West and not in the Rest?" The usual reply was that a certain mode of production (feudalism) or a certain spirit (the Protestant ethic) that would induce capitalism was absent in the Rest. Thus, it is significant to note that Max Weber began his famous book, *The Protestant Ethic and the Spirit of Capitalism*, with the following question of European exceptionalism: "A product of modern European civilization, studying any problem of universal history, is bound to ask himself to what combination of circumstances the fact should be attributed that in Western civilization, and in Western civilization only, cultural phenomena have appeared which (as we like to think) lie in a line of development having *universal* significance and value" (Weber 1976, 13; italics in the original).

In this way, Western social scientists faithfully carried out their task, which was to demonstrate the "fact" that Western civilization was unique and superior, by converting cultural differences that exist–or are supposed to exist–between the West and the Rest into cultural superiority. Likewise, Western social sciences developed rapidly along with the imperialist expansion of European powers. The underlying premise was the *weltanschauung* that represented Western superiority through European exceptionalism and the inferiority of the Rest by way of Orientalism. In this sense, Andre Gunder Frank remarks that European exceptionalism and Orientalism are two sides of the same coin (i.e., Eurocentrism; Frank 1995, 184).

Of course, without exception, the dichotomous scheme based on Eurocentrism was used to compare the West with the Rest in terms of their legal (normative) cultures. That is to say, whereas the West was regulated by law, the Rest was ruled not by law but by the capricious and arbitrary will of individual rulers. Montesquieu, a French enlightenment thinker who became famous for his book *The Spirit of Laws*, formulated the concept "Oriental despotism." He denigrated Persian and other Asian civilizations as areas where the rule of law was absent. He states that, because the peoples of Asia and Africa possessed a servile spirit and lacked the spirit of liberty throughout all periods of their history, despotism–a form of government in which "a single man, unrestrained by law and other rules, dominates by his will and caprices"–reigned supreme outside Europe (quoted in Richter 1977, 196). In his analysis of Confucianism and Daoism, which formed the cultural foundation of China, Max Weber argued that capitalism was not able to develop in China because laws, rational administration and other judicial systems hospitable to it were utterly absent (Weber 1951, 100-104).[3] Thus, major Western intellectuals defined the politics of Asian civilizations, including Persia, India, and China, as Oriental despotism lacking the rule of law. Within Korea, research focusing on the rule of law and the rule of virtue has also been conducted in the shadow of such Eurocentric dichotomies.

Defining Basic Concepts

In this section I shall briefly define the *rule of virtue*, the *rule of* li, the *rule of law*, and *constitutionalism*. First of all, the rule of virtue

3 Long before writing *The Religion of China*, Weber had already stated in *The Protestant Ethic*: "In fact the State itself, in the sense of a political association with a rational, written constitution, rationally ordained law, and an administration bound to rational rules or laws . . . is known . . . only in the Occident despite all other approaches to it" (Weber 1976, 16-17).

is the political principle that seeks to build a peaceful community devoid of crimes and conflicts by inspiring people through the moral influence of virtuous leaders.[4] This idea is based on the premise that people will concede and cooperate with one another only when leaders take the initiative through morally exemplary words and deeds (Lee Seung-hwan 1998, 184). *Li* in Confucianism has dual normative aspects, both behavioral and compulsory. First, *li* works as a "behavioral norm that coordinates the internal relationships among ruling classes, stipulates positions, privileges, property inheritance among various strata, and regulates the daily routines of the common people." But *li* also has the attribute of a compulsory norm in that coercive punishment and execution by public power often accompany a violation (Lee Seoung-hwan 1998, 176). However, many of the clauses in *li*, which the Confucian literati codified and ritualized, were not compulsory norms (in the sense that their violation was not accompanied by punishments), so they could not be regarded properly as laws. Apart from such exceptional clauses, though, the Confucian rule of *li* approaches the rule of law. In this vein, Lee Seung-hwan distinguishes the rule of *li* by Confucians and the rule

4 It cannot be denied that the concept of the rule of virtue in this chapter is defined in a Confucian-centered way. Therefore, there is some difficulty in identifying the rule of virtue in Confucianism with that of Greek political theorists such as Plato and Aristotle. However, whereas the rule of law is primarily concerned with the question "By what mechanism are the people to be governed?," the rule of virtue is mainly interested in the question "What kind of a person should govern the people?" Thus, as the latter is preoccupied with the moral and intellectual qualities of political leaders, there are significant similarities between Greek and Chinese ideas of the rule of virtue in contrast to that of the rule of law. I will disregard some important differences that might exist in the substance of virtue between Greek and Chinese concepts of virtue, as they seem irrelevant at least to the purpose of this chapter.

of law by Legalists by stating that the Confucian *li* corresponds to the law according to natural law, whereas Legalist law corresponds to the law by legal positivists (Lee Seung-hwan 1998, 178). However, most Western scholars and many East Asian scholars have conventionally overlooked the rule-of-law aspect of the rule of *li*, conceptualizing *li* as either moral norms or rituals. In contrast, the "rule of law advocated by Legalists accepted the unlimited rights and power of a king, so that it is no more than an autocratic rule of law in which all the people under him must obey law made by him" (Lee Seung-hwan 1998, 185).[5] This is completely different from the modern Western notion of the rule of law that requires obedience to laws created by an assembly of popularly elected representatives. Thus, the main purpose of the Legalists' rule of law was to strengthen royal power and to control subjects, whereas democratic "rule of law adopted the guarantee of civil rights and the separation of powers as its core principles" (Lee Seung-hwan 1998, 184-85).

Because the rule of law developed in modern Western societies and has come to reign supreme as the universal criterion by which non-Western societies are judged, we need to define the concept in greater detail. Today, the rule of law as one of the core principles of liberal democracy is generally thought to incorporate three main ideas, as A. V. Dicey pointed out a long time ago: "(1) the supremacy of regular laws as opposed to arbitrary power, (2) equality before the law of all persons and classes, including government officials, and (3) the incorporation of constitutional law as a binding part of the

5 For this reason, the rule of law advocated by Legalists is often explained as "rule by law" instead of "rule of law."

ordinary law of the land" (Solum 1994, 111; Gaus 1994, 328-30). Historically, the rule of law in a more traditional sense was understood as referring to the first idea. However, even when the first and second conditions are satisfied, oppressive rule is still possible. For example, if a law banning travel abroad is enacted and applied equally to all, then we can say that the rule of law according to the first two ideas is still valid. Thus, the third idea becomes necessary so that the rule of law may require "a higher or constitutional law that governs ordinary lawmaking, as well as politically independent courts of law to enforce this higher law against public officials" (Macedo 1994, 149). Thus, constitutionalism was added to the rule of law in the modern era. Constitutionalism, together with the guarantee of human rights, the separation of powers, and the existence of a written constitution, are all inseparable parts of the rule of law.[6]

Evolution of the Rule of Law and Its Integration with the Rule of Virtue in the West

The Rule of Law in the History of Western Political Thought

Greek political theorists such as Aristotle; Roman lawyers; the natural law thinkers in the medieval era; modern thinkers such as Locke, Rousseau, Montesquieu, and Hegel; and the Founding

6 Of course, there is a notable exception. England is known to have an unwritten constitution.

Fathers of the United States all generally advocated the rule of law in the historical development of Western political thought. However, because this idea developed in close connection with constitutionalism in the modern era, the rule of law today is commonly examined in terms of constitutionalism.

Western constitutionalism is based on the Greek notion of *politeia*–a "moderate and balanced form of government" or a limited government. Greek *politeia* was also identified "either with the rule of law or the rule of right" as opposed to "the rule of forces" (Maddox 1989, 52). Furthermore, for Aristotle, the rule of law was identified with the rule of God and reason: "He who commands that law should rule may thus be regarded as commanding that God and reason alone should rule; he who commands that a man should rule adds the character of the beast. . . . Law (as the pure voice of God and reason) may thus be defined as Reason free from all passion" (Aristotle 1969, 146). He also maintained that "laws resting on unwritten custom are even more sovereign, and concerned with issues of still more sovereign importance, than written laws" (Aristotle 1969, 147). Thus he attached greater importance to "fundamental laws" (*nomoi*) based on customs than to "assembly laws" (*psephismata*) (Maddox 1989, 53).

At the end of the Roman republic, incorporating and transmitting Greek *political* thought, Cicero coined the term *constitutio*, which then referred to his approximation of the Greek *politeia* and meant a "moderate and balanced form of government" (Maddox 1989, 51). Cicero also imported into Rome the universal law of nature originally developed by the Greek Stoics and raised the "revolutionary notion that wherever the laws of states did not conform with true law–eternal, unchangeable reason–then these particular laws would be invalid." Indeed, his *constitutio* was rule by true law (Maddox 1989, 54-55). Graham Maddox sums up this ancient tradition of the rule of law as follows: "The foundation of Western constitutionalism, therefore, was popular sovereignty, rooted in the nomos of the Greeks, and hallowed in the jurisprudence of the Romans as the rule of right reason deriving from the universal law of nature" (Maddox 1989, 55).

In this way, due to the political traditions and practices of Greece and Rome, the rule of law retained the positive meaning of right rule in connection with popular sovereignty and the law of nature. Thus, whereas the word *constitutio* assumed authoritarian overtones in the long ages after the Roman empire, the rule of law linked to the law of nature retained a positive meaning. The idea that "the king is subject to no person, he is under God and the law" was widely accepted in the medieval age (Maddox 1989, 58).

With the advent of the modern age, however, the idea of the rule of law was revived by the social contract theory based on the law of nature. Notably, John Locke argued for the separation of the legislative and executive powers. He also argued for government through laws made by popularly elected representatives. This rule of law was developed into a full-blown modern constitutional principle through Montesquieu's doctrine of the separation of powers, which sought to guarantee freedom to citizens through checks and balances among the three branches of government: the legislative, the executive, and the judiciary. With the adoption of the American constitution in 1787, the rule of law became established as one of the firmest principles of modern democracy.

However, it should be noted that the ideal of the rule of law did not work effectively in Western societies until full democratization occurred. It was established as one of the basic principles of the governments of England and the United States in the nineteenth century and in other European countries in the early twentieth century. In the meantime, the political reality of the latter was far from the ideal (Dicey 1985, 109-15).

Although it is widely thought that French monarchs before the French Revolution were arbitrary and oppressive, the reality was different. On the contrary, law and public opinion counted for a great deal more than in other European states such as Spain, Germany, and the petty states of Italy (Dicey 1985, 192). Nevertheless, the royal lawlessness of French kings was nothing peculiar, and yet it is an error to suppose that up to 1789 anything like the supremacy of law existed under the French monarchy. The episodes of Voltaire–the most famous Enlightenment thinker of his time–dramatically demonstrate the absence of the rule of law in France. He was sent to the Bastille over a satirical poem he did not author but was thought to have written. Furthermore, the Regent treated the affair as a joke, playing upon the fact the poem described the prison, which Voltaire had never seen. Voltaire had to pay a second visit to the Bastille, for he later complained that lackeys had mocked him at a formal party in the presence of a duke (Dicey 1985, 190). Dicey commented on the lawlessness of France before the Revolution: "A brave officer and a distinguished diplomatist could, for some offence still unknown, without trial and without conviction, be condemned to undergo a penance and disgrace which could hardly be rivaled by the fanciful caprice of the torments inflicted by *Oriental despotism*" (Dicey 1985, 191; emphasis in the original). It is indeed ironic that Dicey applied the concept of Oriental despotism to the home country of Montesquieu, who had originally coined the term to refer to the politics of Asian civilizations. Except for England and the United States, which began earlier to establish the rule of law, the ideal of the rule of law was to be realized on the European continent only after a fierce struggle for democracy over a period of a few hundred years. Its full implementation, however, like democracy, is rather a recent phenomenon.

The Integration of the Rule of Law and the Rule of Virtue in Western Political Thought

It is important to note that the thinkers briefly analyzed in the preceding section did not focus solely on the rule of law. Their idea of the rule of law was reinforced and complemented by the idea of the rule of virtue.

Plato stressed the rule of virtue over the rule of law in his early work, *The Republic*. He suggested rule by philosopher-kings who would pursue the common good of the political community, taking the idea of the Good as their model. Their rule was based on the firm belief in the wisdom of philosophers rather than any codification of it. Thus it approximated an impersonal sophocracy, a variant of the rule of virtue, rather than the rule of law. However, we cannot overlook the fact that there were many constitutional devices in *The Republic* that strictly regulated relations between the rulers and the ruled, as well as the education, recruitment, and living conditions of rulers. In *The Laws*, Plato's final work, though, the rule of law is emphasized. Plato stipulated an elaborate system of laws that included civil and penal codes as well as codes to regulate rulers. However, *The Laws* in the end mandated the power of the Nocturnal Council to make and enforce laws, which shows his ultimate confidence in wise men, thereby adding and institutionalizing the rule of virtue. All this considered, we can conclude that elements of virtue and law coexisted in Plato's legal philosophy, and yet he stressed the rule of virtue more in *The Republic* than in *The Laws* due to his optimistic confidence in the wisdom of philosophers.

Aristotle, who was influenced more by Plato's *The Laws* than by *The Republic*, stressed the rule of law more than the rule of virtue. Discussing the rule of law in contrast to the rule of men, however, he did not give up rule by the best man. Examining various types of kingship in *The Politics*, he posed the following question: "Is it more expedient to be ruled by the one best man, or by the best laws?" (Aristotle 1969, 141). In the end, he found that the rule of unwritten law was the safest, and the rule of a man–the single best man–might be safer than the rule of written law (Aristotle 1969, 147).[7] He was worried that the element of passion in the rule of a man would disturb human reason. However, when individual rulers were needed to cope with something that the law had not anticipated, Aristotle said that "they should be made 'law-guardians' or ministers of the law who applied the spirit of the law to concrete cases" (Aristotle 1969, 146).

7 However, in the case of the rule of the single best man, Aristotle maintains that the general principle must also be present in the ruler's mind (Aristotle 1969, 141).

In *Ethics*, Aristotle developed this idea further, suggesting the concept of equity to fill the gap between general law and concrete reality. He made some room for the judge's discretionary power in interpreting the law (Aristotle 1976, 199). This position, which attaches importance to the application of equity in contemporary Western jurisprudence, also tends to stress judicial virtues and the moral education of judges to prevent the abuse and misuse of equity (Solum 1994). Here we cannot deny that such a judicial position that stresses the equity and discretionary power of a judge overlaps with the rule of virtue stressed by Confucians, as will be examined later.

It is clear that such a position takes advantage of the rule of virtue to supplement the flaws in the rule of law rather than acknowledge the superiority of the rule of virtue. However, some strong strands of the rule of virtue existed in Aristotelian notions of the rule of law. He valued unwritten over written law and identified the rule of law with that of God and reason. This seems to indicate that for him the rule of law was more opposed to the rule of men than to the rule of virtue.

Evolution of the Rule of Law and Its Integration with the Rule of Virtue in East Asia

Conventional Status of the Rule of Law in the History of East Asian Political Thought

In contrast to the West, the rule of law has not been considered the proper and desirable principle of government in East Asian civilization. Law and the rule of law have been perceived negatively in the historical tradition of Chinese political thought. The causes for such a negative perception are threefold. First, Legalists actively promoted a rule of law that stressed strict and heavy punishment to attain a rich state and strong army. Second, the Qin empire, which first unified China with the help of the Legalists, ruled rather harshly, causing its people great grief. Third, the Han empire, which succeeded the Qin, adopted as the state religion Confucianism, which was very critical of the Legalist rule of law.

However, it is important to note that law (*fa*) was a concept with various meanings from the Zhou dynasty until the Warring States period and did not initially have the overly negative connotations it later acquired. Originally having the meaning "assessing crimes and imposing punishments," meanings for the word *law* also included "model," "type," "formula," "frame," "standard," and "institution" (Chang Hyeon-geun 1994, 77-79). With the appearance of the earlier Legalists, the meaning of *law* was enriched and it came to denote a "political institution in general (to govern the relationships between the king and subjects, and between superiors and inferiors)," "the standard by which to judge the propriety of words and practices of subjects," "codes of rewards and punishments" to govern the people, and "economic-related regulations," including clauses to secure the uniformity of measures and scales (Chang Hyeon-geun 1994, 89-90).

However, with the Legalists coming to power as advisors to kings and lords in the later Warring States period, the negative connotations of law and the rule of law coincided closely with the process in which the originally rich meanings of law had undergone extreme reduction to punishments and rewards.[8] Thus, law had to be relegated to a subsidiary status to assist the Confucian ideal of the rule of virtue and politics as education in the Han empire when Confucians came to power. This was a cultural triumph over the Legalists for the Confucians. However, the price paid was dear: the meaning of law was reduced to punishments and rewards, and the rule of law was relegated to mere instrumental status in all periods of Chinese history that followed. As a result, the rule of virtue and *li* came to be respected as proper rule, whereas the rule of law was stigmatized as an evil rule, as demonstrated by the following brief analysis of *The Confucian Analects, The Works of Mencius, Xunzi,* and *The Works of Han Fei Tzu.*

We can observe in a famous passage from *The Confucian Analects* that Confucius criticized the rule of law in the narrow sense of the term; that is, perceived mainly as punishments and prohibition. Instead, he stressed the rule of virtue: "If the people be led by decrees (prohibitions), and uniformity sought to be given them by punishments, they will try to avoid the punishment, but have no sense of shame. If they be led by virtue, and uniformity sought to be given them by the rules of propriety (*li*), they will have the sense of shame, and moreover will become good" (Confucius 1960, 146). This passage has commonly been interpreted as Confucius's opposition to the rule of law. However, scholars have recently presented a revised interpretation. They emphasize the superiority of the rule of virtue

8 Thus, the original meaning of *fa* was very close to that of *law* in English. However, *fa* reduced primarily to punishments and rewards does not correspond to the English word *law*.

over the rule of law, especially in terms of the role of politics as education, rather than entirely rejecting the latter. In this regard, we need to remember that Confucianism has traditionally stressed the combination of propriety-music-punishment-prohibition as the means of normative control over people. This is to acknowledge that coercive norms are indispensable to politics. Thus, propriety and music purify humans internally, whereas punishment and prohibition control human behavior externally (Lee Sang-ik 2001, 259-60).

However, it should also be noted that, according to Confucius, the word *law* referred to political institutions in general and never to compulsory norms such as punishments and prohibition. When Confucius praises the political achievements of King Tang, he states, "He carefully attended to the weights and measures, examined the body of the laws, restored the discarded officers, and the good government of the kingdom took its course" (Confucius 1960, 351). He also teaches elsewhere in *The Confucian Analects*: "Can men refuse to assent to the words of laws and reason?" (Confucius 1960, 224). From such passages we can infer that Confucius used the word *law* in a positive sense to refer to political institutions in general or to an exemplary model.

Mencius also stressed benevolent rule and criticized rulers for inflicting punishment without securing an adequate livelihood for the people and teaching them beforehand: "When they have thus been involved in crime, to follow them up and punish them–this is to entrap the people. How can such a thing as entrapping the people be done under the rule of a benevolent man?" (Mencius 1960, 240). Thus, it is clear that he also stressed benevolent rule, opposing the rule of law that primarily focused on punishment. In fact, Mencius regarded benevolent rule as the objective standard of politics, playing a similar role to the compass and square for carpenters and the tuning fork for musicians (Mencius 1960, 288). It is also significant to note that the word *law* is never used in a negative sense throughout *The Works of Mencius*, as the following passages demonstrate. Explaining to a duke the educational institutions for the instruction of the people and the nine-square system of dividing the land during the previous dynasties, Mencius states, "Should a real sovereign arise, he will certainly come and take these laws from you; and thus you will be the teacher of the true sovereign" (Mencius 1960, 243; translation revised). In another passage, he states, "Hence we have the saying: 'Virtue alone is not sufficient for the exercise of government; laws alone cannot carry themselves into practice'" (Mencius 1960, 289). All these passages suggest that *laws* referred to the political institution in general in a positive sense. Sometimes *laws* referred to principles, models, and examples (Mencius 1960, 288, 290-91). In short, Confucius and Mencius used the word *law* in a positive manner to refer to political institutions, norms, models, and so forth, while criticizing the rule of law in the narrow sense when it relied on coercive means such as punishment.

However, the elements of rewards and punishments in the concept of law became more predominant as the influence of the Legalists grew during the later period of the Warring States. Xunzi, although a Confucian, stressed *li* (ritual principles) and punishment as the basis of politics and began to assess the rule of law in the narrow sense as well as assessing the rule of ritual principles in a more positive light than Confucius and Mencius. For Xunzi, who is well known for his emphasis of the rule of *li*, the concept of *li* now gained particular significance as the standard of politics, instead of Mencius's benevolent rule (Xunzi 1988, vol. 3, 177). Xunzi identified *li* with law in a wider sense, arguing that ritual principles were the basis of laws (Xunzi 1988, vol. 1, 139) and that, of the sources of ritual principles, none is more important than the laws and reason of the sage kings (Xunzi 1988, vol. 1, 157, 206). However, the following passages show that he also approved of the importance of the rule of law in the narrow sense espoused by the Legalists:

> People will then clearly perceive that good, though performed in the privacy of the home, will be selected for commendation in the royal court and that acts contrary to the good, though performed in darkest secrecy, will be exposed to punishment in public view. This may be described as "having fixed principles." Such are the principles of a king. (Xunzi 1988, vol. 2, 101)

> Where the government and punishments are equitable, people are attracted to make their home there. Where ritual and moral principles are perfected, the gentleman will be attracted to make his home there. (Xunzi 1988, vol. 2, 206)

> Accordingly, if there is to be order, then punishments must be heavy, and if there is to be chaos, then punishments must be light. The treatment of criminal offenders in a period of good government is sternly harsh, and their treatment in a chaotic

> age is exceedingly light. (Xunzi 1988, vol. 3, 38)

Still, he firmly maintained his Confucian identity by repeatedly stressing that rule by exemplary action through benevolence, righteousness, and ritual principles was superior to the rule of law in the narrow sense and that a gentleman, as the central agent of the rule of virtue and ritual principles, was the essential ingredient that binds together the Way and the law. He stated the superiority of Confucian *li* to law or force as follows:

> A lord of men who exalts ritual principles and honors worthy men will become a True King; one who stresses law and loves the people will become lord-protector; one who is fond of profit and is much given to dissimulation will be imperiled; and one who schemes after power, plots revolution, and risks secret intrigues will perish. (Xunzi 1988, vol. 3, 20)

Turning to the earlier Legalists, laws retained the nature of moral norms, referring to social customs and political institutions in general (Chang Hyeon-geun 1994, 85-88). However, by the age of Han Fei Tzu, their meaning was reduced to the narrow sense of punishments and rewards. Law as merely a governing tool was brought into sharp relief. This is easily confirmed in the following passages: "[The king] must control his subjects by state laws" (Han Fei Tzu 1999, 32), and "the high ministers resented their laws and the common people hated orderly government" (Han Fei Tzu 1999, 104). Whereas Xunzi recognized the importance of both ritual principles with educative functions and laws in the narrow sense, Han Fei Tzu conceived of benevolence and righteousness as opposed to laws: "A king who has mastered statecraft keeps himself distant from benevolence and righteousness, overlooks prudence and wisdom, and follows only laws and institutions" (Han Fei Tzu 1999, 466). Whereas benevolent politics were the compass and square for Confucius and Mencius, as ritual principles were for Xunzi, Han Fei Tzu's compass and square was the law in the narrow sense–punishments and rewards: "If an ordinary king observes the law and institutions and a poor artisan applies the measure, there will be no mistake either in state affairs or in carpentry. Thus a king as such . . . will accomplish a great deed if he puts efforts to apply the method by which an ordinary artisan should not make a mistake" (Han Fei Tzu 1999, 244).

It is natural, then, that Han Fei Tzu criticized the utility of the rule of benevolence and ritual principles. He argued that people would become licentious and disorderly if a ruler treated them with benevolence (Han Fei Tzu 1999, 496). Few would do good things inspired by a sage, yet many would restrain from doing evils when scared by laws (Han Fei Tzu 1999, 533). Furthermore, benevolent rule espoused by Confucians would become impossible in an age of increased population with relatively scarce goods, even though it might have been possible in the age of Kings Yao and Shun when people were scarce and goods were sufficient (Han Fei Tzu 1999, 512-13).

It is difficult to deny that the Legalists, who emphasized rewards and punishments as instruments of statecraft and the notion of a rich state and strong army, contributed to Qin's unification. In addition,

Han Fei Tzu suggested the expansion of some positive aspects of the rule of law; he demanded that laws be displayed in public offices, and he proclaimed to the populace that hard-to-obey laws would not be made and that laws would be applied equally regardless of status. Nevertheless, the critical flaw in his idea was that he did not come up with any institutions or devices to serve as checks against the arbitrary will of rulers, although his idea of the rule of law assumed their mediocrity. Thus, his idea would inevitably lead to the acceptance of tyranny because there were no institutional mechanisms to prevent those rulers, who were to be armed with the laws of punishments and rewards as well as influence and trickery, from whimsically wielding power. Finally and most important, Han Fei Tzu decisively contributed to the reduction of law to mere punishments and rewards, as well as to its negative connotation in the history of Chinese political thought. To intellectuals as well as to the general populace, the rule of law as such came to symbolize the model of oppressive rule originating from the Qin empire.

The Integration of the Rule of Law and the Rule of Virtue: The Case of Confucius and Mencius

I have argued thus far that Confucius and Mencius placed more emphasis on the rule of virtue and *li*, approved of the rule of law in the wide sense, and did not reject the rule of law in the narrow sense of punishments and rewards.[9] However, there are certain passages

9 In this section, I shall not discuss Xunzi, for the rule of *li* and the rule of law existed side by side in *Xunzi*, or Han Fei Tzu, for he was vehemently opposed to the rule of virtue.

in *The Confucian Analects* and *The Works of Mencius* that are likely to be interpreted as opposing the narrow sense of the rule of law. Therefore, I shall present my own interpretations of these passages to demonstrate that they may not only be reconciled with the rule of law in the narrow sense but also adapted to the modern idea of the rule of law. The purpose of this section is to clearly demonstrate that their legal philosophy, which is based on the rule of virtue, is fully compatible with the modern rule of law.

First of all, we can see in the following passage that Confucius recognized law in the narrow sense (i.e., legal punishment) as positive or neutral: "The superior man thinks of virtue; the small man thinks of comfort. The superior man thinks of the sanctions of law; the small man thinks of favors which he may receive" (Confucius 1960, 168). This passage indicates that the gentleman takes into consideration punishments as well as benevolence and virtue when determining his conduct. In addition, Confucius did not deny the need for litigation, although he aimed at its ultimate abolition: "In hearing litigations, I am competent like anybody. What is necessary, however, is to cause the people to have no litigations" (Confucius 1960, 257). This passage suggests that, although he did not deny the positive function of litigation, it was not his cherished ideal.

Moreover, it seems inadequate to interpret the famous dialogue between the Duke of Sheh and Confucius as the latter's opposition to the rule of law. In the dialogue in which they debated whether it was good for a son to reveal his father's theft to the public authorities, the duke praised the son as a righteous man, whereas Confucius refused to consider him righteous. The latter view has been commonly interpreted as Confucius's opposition to the rule of law. However, this debate only suggests that in the conflict between filial piety and loyalty (to the king), Confucius stressed the priority of filial piety, whereas the duke emphasized loyalty. This should not be interpreted as Confucius opposing the proper execution of law for the father nor condoning the son's probable resistance against a public official who came to arrest his father. In this episode, it is not clear yet whether the son was legally obligated to report the father's theft to the authorities. In connection with this, it should be noted that the contemporary penal code does not punish the harboring of criminals or nonreporting of criminals when his or her family members or close relatives are the perpetrators. In this regard, the modern Rechtsstaat, which is supposed to give higher priority to law and order over family ties, makes an important concession. It is also clear that Confucius would be willing to endorse such a provision. Furthermore, it suggests that public authorities who give priority to the public over the private cannot but honor the primacy of certain private relations by withholding the application of state laws in some exceptional circumstances.

An episode that Han Fei Tzu cited to criticize Confucius's conduct should also not be interpreted as the latter's opposition to the rule of law. In this episode, rather than punishing a soldier who had deserted three times to support his elderly father, Confucius allegedly set him free and rewarded him with a good position (Han Fei Tzu 1999, 518-19). It is true that in this case Confucius condoned the soldier's violation of the law and that he was not a legal positivist who demanded unconditional obedience to positive law. However, we cannot say that there is no way to protect such a soldier even according to the modern principle of the rule of law or according to the logic of legal positivism. In this case, although positive law binds a judge, by considering the extenuating circumstances, Confucius as a judge might be able to release him with a suspension of his sentence. In a modern constitutional democracy, he would be able to challenge the constitutionality of the military service act that enlists a person whose elderly parents have to rely upon him for their subsistence, or to request a judicial review of the act by a constitutional court. There was no such constitutional device in the time of Confucius. However, it does seem quite clear that a judge possessed broad discretionary power in those early times, so that he could release a defendant without punishment. Such a situation allows us to think that no laws were violated. As such, the episode does not prove that Confucius was against the rule of law. Through the reinterpretation of these two episodes, therefore, we can find that the Confucian ideal of the ethical order can be accommodated to fit the contemporary rule of law.

Mencius also stressed the integration of the rule of virtue and the rule of law in the same spirit as Confucius, as I noted earlier. However, a frequently cited case is commonly interpreted as his opposition to the rule of law (Mencius 1960, 469-70). Mencius was asked how King Shun would have acted if his father had committed a homicide and the minister of justice was about to arrest him. This question is similar to the one Confucius faced in the aforementioned case–a clash between loyalty interpreted as obedience to the law of the country and filial piety. Mencius replied that whereas the minister would have executed the law soberly, Shun would have been willing to abdicate the throne without any hesitation, escape to a remote seashore carrying his father on his back, and live there forgetting worldly affairs. Here Mencius's reply has been viewed conventionally as the evidence showing his disregard of the law. However, if we scrutinize Shun's hypothetical action in Mencius's reply, Shun would have had the minister execute the law, thereby stressing equality before the law regardless of status. Although Shun's escape with his father did not accord with the law, the rule of law was not violated and was somehow respected, in the sense that Shun gave up his throne to become a private person without attempting to abuse his office by escaping the law and thereby exempting himself from performing his public duty. Now the rest of the story amounts to the question: "What if a son should hide his father who committed a crime?" This is the familiar question that was already examined with regard to Confucius's dialogue.

Considering all this together, we need to note that Confucius and Mencius sought to oppose or suspend the application of positive laws to protect ethical values. In the three cases examined here, the value was filial piety and the laws opposed or suspended were criminal laws. The basic spirit of protecting such values by suspending the laws of the country when they threatened to infringe upon the rights of the populace fully accords with an important aspect of the contemporary rule of law–the protection of civil rights and liberties. The words and deeds of Confucius and Mencius in these three cases are consistent with Confucius's saying quoted earlier: "The populace should be governed first by virtue and propriety." If the actors in the three cases had been accused of crimes of nonreporting, harboring criminals, or deserting from the military according to the strict application of the law, they would not have felt ashamed of themselves regardless of the actual outcomes–whether they were convicted or acquitted. Should they have been found guilty, they would have felt aggrieved or resentful of the law. Moreover, it is clear that positive laws that punish such acts clash head-on with the Confucian principle of "for the people" as well as the ethical order Confucians cherish. In addition, their punishment would correspond to the case in which Confucius criticized laws that injured benevolence: "When punishments are not properly awarded, the people do not know how to move hand or foot" (Confucius 1960, 264). Thus, we can conclude that even the limited cases in which Confucius and Mencius seem to have opposed the rule of law in favor of benevolent rule are not only compatible with, but also welcomed by, the contemporary rule of law.

Contemporary Constitutionalism and the Confucian Constitutionalism of *Li* in East Asia

When we compare the Chinese legal philosophies of Confucianism and Legalism with the modern Western rule of law, we find that Legalism stresses the first two aspects of the modern rule of law–the supremacy of laws and equality before the law.[10] In contrast, Confucianism does not acknowledge the supremacy of the positive law and denies equality before the law, because it approves of the discriminatory treatment of people according to status. However,

10 In this section I have drawn heavily upon Hahm Chaihark's work in general and his concept of ritualist constitutionalism in particular. See Hahm Chaihark (2000) for more details.

Confucian legal philosophy has maintained an unusual and consistent concern with the third element of the rule of law–the constitutional problem of how to control rulers. Above all else, Confucianism has stressed the moral discipline of rulers and especially the education of the people through the rule of virtue. Confucian ideas of the "people as the basis" and "for the people" also emphasize benevolent rule. In Confucianism, only rulers who rule benevolently can attain legitimacy as true leaders. Thus, the constitutional spirit has been internalized in Confucian philosophy, such as in the rule of virtue, the mandate of Heaven, the idea of "for the people," and so forth.

In the history of Western political thought, constitutionalist thought developed by focusing on popular sovereignty, the idea of a mixed constitution, and the rule of law as the collective will of the community or the law of nature. Thus, constitutionalism has evolved in close relationship with the rule of law. Moreover, it has attained a strong status with the liberal-democratic addition of human rights and the separation of powers. However, in East Asian civilization with China at its center, the situation was different. Concerns about controlling a ruler's arbitrary power and protecting the rights of the people did not develop in relation to the rule of law, for the law was reduced to the mere tools of a ruler; that is, punishments and rewards.

Of course, successive dynasties in China filed and published elaborate codes of laws and decrees, according to the principle of "Confucianism on the outside and Legalism in the inside" in the Han dynasty. This, in turn, promoted the simultaneous trends of the Confucianization of law and the legalization of Confucian *li* beginning in the Han dynasty. Notable examples are the *Tang Liudian*

(Six Canons of Tang), *Da Ming Huidian* (Collected Canons of the Great Ming), *Da Qing Huidian* (Collected Canons of Great Qing), and so forth. These codes included administrative laws (*dian*)–the assignment and division of government offices and the distribution of their elaborate jurisdictions and authorities–as well as penal laws and other laws regulating civil and commercial affairs. Looking into these codes carefully, we find that the first two elements of the modern rule of law took shape as basic principles. Therefore, some sophisticated Western scholars have argued that East Asian civilization lacked the notion of constitutionalism in the sense that there have never been any explicit constitutional institutions or norms to regulate rulers.

However, if we examine the Confucian rule of *li* more closely, we can recognize some significant elements that correspond to Western constitutionalism, albeit not liberal in form. In this regard, it is important to remember that constitutional elements, which had previously been incorporated into the law in a wider sense, were transferred into the concept of *li* when Legalists reduced the meaning of law to mere punishments and rewards. We also have to pay special attention to the legalization of *li*, for it stresses the idea of regulating the activities of all government actors, such as disciplining rulers, whereas the Confucianization of law has to do with promoting Confucian values among the populace through coercive means (Hahm Chaihark 2000, 126-27). The traditional East Asian constitutional framework comprises three parts: ritual (*li*), administrative (*dian*), and penal (*leu*). Hahm Chaihark has argued that among the three, *li* should be seen as the constitutional norm, for they were indeed a regularized restraint on the rulers (Hahm Chaihark 2000, 112).

Some parts of the Great Canons, when referring to *li*, stipulated detailed clauses that regulated the ritual processes of a monarch's conduct and the proper rituals to be observed between monarchs and ministers. Thus, we should note that *li*'s most important function was to regulate human behavior from without and to restrain it from within. That disciplinary function of *li* was explicitly recognized in *The Confucian Analects*: "Look not at what is contrary to propriety; listen not to what is contrary to propriety; speak not what is contrary to propriety; make no movement which is contrary to propriety" (Confucius 1960, 250).[11] As the ritual the rulers had to follow had been codified since the Han empire, the function of *li* in disciplining rulers was reinforced (Hahm Chaihark 2000, 127). In addition, *dian*–the administrative law, which regulated the administrative process–played a constitutional function as well. Thus, if rulers did not observe proper rituals, they were perceived as having lost their legitimacy as rulers in China and the Joseon Korea (1392-1910).

Thus, following Hahm Chaihark's interpretation, we can conceive of *li* as a political norm, taking an intermediate form between law and morals, that played a constitutional role in restraining rulers in a regularized form. In England and the United States, constitutionalism was accomplished by subjecting the exercise of political power to the jurisdiction of the court. In that process, the rule of law was fully developed and strengthened. However, the constitutional system in China and the Joseon dynasty conceived of

11 Elsewhere in *The Confucian Analects*, the philosopher Yu says of *li*: "In practicing the rules of propriety, a natural ease is to be prized. In the ways prescribed by the ancient kings, this is the excellent quality, and in things small and great we follow them" (Confucius 1960, 143).

political power as ritualist and sought to regulate rulers through *li* as much as possible, so that the exercise of a ruler's political power was strongly subjected to *li*. In that process, the "way of the ancient sage kings" such as Yao, Shun, or Duke of Zhou, and "the way of the former kings" and "ancestral laws" were effective in regulating a ruler's behavior.

Such constitutional ideas were institutionalized most systematically and effectively in the Joseon dynasty, which sought to carry out Confucian ideals to the fullest degree among East Asian countries. If we make a brief summary of these institutional arrangements, we may cite the "prime minister," "royal lectures," "institutionalized remonstrance," and "court historians" as notable examples. In addition to these, the famous ritual controversies among political partisans in the Joseon dynasty may be duly interpreted as a proper form of constitutional debate over the issues, some of which were directly related to how to control kings and royal families (for more details, see Hahm Chaihark 2000).

Conclusion

Our examination of the development of the rule of law and the rule of virtue in the history of Western and East Asian political thought, albeit sketchy, has shown that the general position of the two civilizations was not to take the one and to exclude the other, but to integrate the two. This is because most political thinkers of the East and West were soberly aware of the modern legal predicament that the rule of law alone would not be fully realized without the spirit of law-abidingness. In turn, law-abidingness is a product of the rule of virtue, which imbues citizens with civic virtues and positive habits. The Confucian emphasis on the rule of virtue also comes from the same concern. Confucius, though he once claimed to respect the political institutions and affairs of the Zhou dynasty, saying, "I shall follow Zhou," stressed the rule of virtue to mitigate the overly legalistic and elaborate aspects of the Zhou legal system. He might have been fully aware that to assert the rule of law in times of extreme confusion and chaos such as in the Spring and Autumn period would seem quite utopian. Nevertheless, the reason he adhered to such a bold philosophy is that he firmly believed it was impossible to secure the observance of social norms among the populace–not to mention their moral improvement–only by building elaborate institutions, especially for punishment and prohibition. This also came from his belief that the rule of virtue, aside from its function as an idealist goal, should constitute part of our reality by being constantly applied as a criterion by which we are to interpret and criticize that reality.

References

English Materials

Aristotle. 1969. *The Politics of Aristotle.* Edited and translated by Ernest Barker. Oxford: Oxford University Press.

——. 1976. *Ethics.* Harmondsworth: Penguin.

Barker, Ernest. 1959. *The Political Thought of Plato and Aristotle.* New York: Dover Publications.

Confucius. 1960. *The Confucian Analects.* Vol. 1 of *The Chinese Classics,* edited and translated by James Legge, 137-354. Hong Kong: Hong Kong University Press.

Dicey, Albert. V. 1985. *An Introduction to the Study of the Law of the Constitution.* 10th ed. London: Macmillan.

Frank, Andre Gunder. 1995. "The Modern World System Revisited: Rereading Braudel and Wallerstein." In *Civilizations and World Systems: Studying World-Historical Change,* edited by Stephen K. Sanderson, 163-94. Walnut Creek, CA: AltaMira Press.

Gaus, Gerald F. 1994. "Public Reason and the Rule of Law." In *The Rule of Law: Nomos XXVI,* 328-55.

Hahm, Chaihark. 2000. "Confucian Constitutionalism." JSD diss., Harvard Law School.

Macedo, Stephen. 1994. "The Rule of Law, Justice, and the Politics of Moderation." In *The Rule of Law: Nomos XXVI,* 148-77.

Maddox, Graham. 1989. "Constitution." In *Political Innovation and Conceptual Change,* edited by Terrence Ball, 50-67. Cambridge: Cambridge University Press.

Mencius. 1960. *The Works of Mencius*. Vol. 2 of *The Chinese Classics: The Works of Mencius*, edited and translated by James Legge. Hong Kong: Hong Kong University Press.

Plato. 1980. *The Laws*. Harmondsworth: Penguin.

Richter, Melvin. 1977. *The Political Theory of Montesquieu*. Cambridge: Cambridge University Press.

Shapiro, Ian, ed. 1994. *The Rule of Law: Nomos XXVI*. New York: New York University Press.

Solum, Lawrence B. 1994. "Equity and the Rule of Law." In Ian Shapiro, 1994, 120-47.

Weber, Max. 1951. *The Religion of China*. Glencoe, IL: The Free Press.

——. 1976. *The Protestant Ethic and the Spirit of Capitalism*. New York: Charles Scribner.

Xunzi. 1988. *Xunzi: A Translation and Study of the Complete Works*. Edited and translated by John Knoblock. 3 vols. Stanford: Stanford University Press.

Korean Materials

Chang, Hyeon-geun. 1994. "Seonjinjeongchisasangeseo Beobui Uimi" [The Meaning of Law in Pre-Qin Political Thought]. *Hangukjeongchihakoebo* [Korean Political Science Review] 27 (2): 75-96.

Hanbija [Han Fei Tzu]. 1999. *Hanbija* [The Works of Han Fei Tzu]. Edited and translated by Geon-young Park and Won-gyu Lee. Seoul: Chunga Publishing Co.

Lee, Sang-ik. 2001. *Yuga Sahoecheolhak Yeongu* [A Study of Confucian Social Philosophy]. Seoul: Simsan.

Lee, Seung-hwan. 1998. *Yugasasangui Sahoecheolhakjeok Jaejomyeong* [A

Reexamination of Confucian Social Philosophy]. Seoul: Korea University Press.

GLOSSARY

dian (Ch.) 典

fa (Ch.) 法

leu (Ch.) 律

li (Ch.) 禮

(Ch.: Chinese)

Chapter 4

Comparative Analysis of Eastern and Western Tyranny: Focusing on Aristotle and Mencius

Westcentrism,[1] which has been developed in close association with Hegelian historicism since the Enlightenment, underlies liberalism and Marxism, created by modern European civilization as universal political ideologies. It has also served as the core assumption of modernization theory since World War II and of the civilizing mission of European colonialism and imperialism in the nineteenth century. In the evolution of Westcentrism, modern Western thinkers took advantage of the intellectual heritage of ancient

1 *Eurocentrism* is used more frequently than *Westcentrism*. This chapter will use the latter term to explicitly include the United States, Canada, Australia, and so on. Westcentrism consists of three general propositions. First, modern Western civilization has reached the highest stage of development in human history (Western superiority). Second, the developmental stages in Western history are universally applicable to all human histories in the world (universalism and historicism). Third, non-Western societies positioned in lower stages of development in history can improve themselves only by emulating and accepting Western civilization (civilization/modernization = Westernization).

Greek civilization, which they called upon as their ancestor, so that Greek philosophers unwittingly influenced the shaping of modern Westcentrism. For example, in his examination of tyranny in *The Politics*, which would later become a classic of Western political science, Aristotle described tyranny as originating from and therefore suitable for Asia. Later Enlightenment thinkers in Europe embarked on a mission to reappropriate the Aristotelian, Hellenocentric coupling of Asia and tyranny and to elaborate it in the Westcentric concept of "Oriental despotism," which was fully formulated by Montesquieu. Thus, the Aristotelian concept of tyranny based on a Hellenocentric version of civilization-barbarism was inherited and expanded in Montesquieu's notion of Oriental despotism. Montesquieu stated that because the peoples of Asia and Africa possessed a servile spirit and lacked the spirit of liberty throughout their entire history, despotism–a form of government in which "a single man, unrestrained by law and other rules, dominate[d] by his will and caprices"–reigned supreme outside Europe (quoted in Richter 1977, 196, 214).[2] In addition, John Stuart Mill, who completed the development of modern liberalism, asserted that Asians had never undertaken any form of systematic resistance against ruling power, so Asian civilizations had repeated a cycle of stagnation and decay (Lee Seung-hwan 1998, 82).

Western bias against Asian civilization in the era of imperialism

2 In opposition to this Orientalist attitude, one interpretation notes that the rule of virtue and the rule of law (or ritual/propriety) were closely intertwined in classical Confucianism represented by Confucius, Mencius, and Xunzi. Also, the rule of *li* (ritual/propriety) in Confucianism was actually a nonliberal form of constitutionalism related to the constitutional issue of how to control rulers. See Kang Jung In (2003).

and colonialism has seemed to find contemporary reverberation with regard to the prospects of democracy in East Asia; for example, in the argument of Samuel P. Huntington. He noted that Confucian democracy was a contradiction in terms because Confucian tradition was hostile to democracy. Thus Huntington (1991) asserted in his survey of democratization in non-Western societies of the late twentieth century that Confucianism was a more critical barrier to democracy than Islam, whereas Christianity encouraged the development of democracy. In this context, Montesquieu's assertion that tyranny reigned supreme in Asia correlates with the Aristotelian understanding that Asia presents an archetypal example of tyranny. Also, Mill's assertion that Asian history lacks systematic resistance is a modern version of the Aristotelian approach claiming that the people of Asia are servile and therefore take tyrannical rule for granted. Furthermore, Huntington's characterization of Confucianism as hostile to democracy and democracy in East Asia as "dominant-party democracy" suggests, too, that authoritarianism, a contemporary substitute for tyranny, is acceptable and natural in East Asia, whereas democracy therein is unstable and deviant.[3] Considering the line of thought from Aristotle to Huntington, we can see that Westcentrism has been deeply rooted in the Western intellectual tradition for more than two thousand years and emerged later in a full-blown form to legitimate Western imperialism and colonialism in the modern era.

3 At the same time, it may be said that democracy in the West is normal and natural, whereas Nazism, Fascism, and Franco's authoritarianism appear to have been temporary perversions. With regard to the critique of Western scholars' (particularly Huntington's) Westcentrism with regard to democracy, see Kang Jung In (1999, 2000).

The purpose of this chapter is to refute the perennial assumption held by Western thinkers and scholars such as Aristotle, Montesquieu, Mill, and Huntington. The chapter will show that there has been a strong tradition in Confucian political thought that criticizes and resists tyranny and even justifies revolting against it. We will first examine the Aristotelian notion of tyranny in order to find out how tyranny and Asia were combined in Aristotle's nascent form of Orientalism. Next, we shall compare Aristotle's analysis of tyranny with the political thought of Mencius in order to prove that there has also been a great tradition in the Confucianism of East Asia to check and control tyranny.[4] This comparison will show that the Westcentric concept of Oriental despotism, which appeared in a pristine form in Aristotle and has been inherited and expanded by modern and contemporary Western thinkers since Montesquieu, might not apply to the Confucian tradition of East Asia. We will even show that, in fact, resistance against oppression and tyranny is an active component in Confucian tradition.

This insight might be useful in forming a united intellectual front of East and West to resist contemporary tyranny. Today, Orientalist thought still stubbornly haunts the world, dividing it into a dichotomy of civilization and barbarism as well as asserting that authoritarianism, a modern substitute for tyranny, is natural and normal in the East, whereas democracy is natural and normal in the West. Also, by comparing Aristotle's theory on the politics of city-states with Mencius, who lived in the Warring States period of pre-

4 Aristotle lived from 384 to 322 BCE and Mencius from 372 to 289 BCE–the two men lived almost in the same period.

Qin China, this discussion proves a preliminary kind of dialogue among civilizations.

Hellenocentric Orientalism in Aristotle's Concept of Tyranny

Aristotle wrote *The Politics* by collecting materials from the Greek polis and neighboring states and by empirically analyzing and comparing their political systems. Although *The Politics* is still considered one of the greatest books in politics, the book reflects a pristine form of Orientalism. This refers to Aristotle's Hellenocentric worldview (and the conventional view of the time) that Greek citizens, living freely in a self-governing polis, had developed reason to the fullest degree and had reached the highest stage of human development. Although his research method was objective and empirical, Aristotle erred in defining the differences between the Greeks and the neighboring tribes as natural and essential[5] and presenting the "other" as barbarian. Aristotle's *The Politics* sets the Greeks against the Persians through Hellenocentric exceptionalism

5 As we shall later examine, Aristotle defines human nature as essentialist in terms of ethnic differences. According to *Key Concepts in Post-Colonial Studies*, "Essentialism is the assumption that groups, categories or classes of objects have one or several defining features exclusive to all members of that category. Some studies of race or gender, for instance, assume the presence of essential characteristics distinguishing one race from another or the feminine from the masculine. In analyses of culture it is a (generally implicit) assumption that individuals share an essential cultural identity" (Ashcroft, Griffiths, and Tiffin 1998, 77).

and Orientalism. Contemporary Westcentrism has inherited and expanded this Hellenocentric attitude, adopting ancient Greek civilization as its intellectual origin and thus identifying Hellenocentrism as its archetype.

Therefore, we need to examine how tyranny and Asia were coupled in Aristotle's political thought. In the beginning of *The Politics*, Aristotle distinguishes the rule of a statesman from those of a monarch and a house manager (a patriarch). The rule of a statesman as a horizontal ruler over free and equal citizens is basically democratic in the sense that the ruler exercises "his authority in conformity with the rules imposed by the art of statesmanship and as one who rules and is ruled in turn" (Aristotle 1969, 1-2). In contrast, the rule of a monarch and a patriarch as the vertical one over unfree and unequal humans are basically despotic in the sense they wield an "uncontrolled and sole authority" (Aristotle 1969, 1).

Aristotle distinguishes between Greeks and barbarians, the latter including both Europeans and Asians (Persians). That is to say, the ancient Greeks felt themselves distinct from Europeans and Asians. The Greek stock belonged to the natural master and ruling element, as it had the capacity, "by virtue of its intelligence, to exercise forethought" (Aristotle 1969, 3). By contrast, the barbarian stock was in a state of slavery by nature, because it lacked a natural ruling element and had "the element which was able, by virtue of its bodily power, to do the physical work" (Aristotle 1969, 3). Thus, the barbarians and the slaves are the same by nature. Aristotle quotes the following phrase from a poem: "barbarous peoples should be governed by the Greeks" (Aristotle 1969, 3). It was natural for the ancient Greeks to think that they were equipped with rational faculty and freedom that allowed them to participate in the political life of the polis, their supreme political association. The polis, the civilized political community, was supposed to pursue the common interest of free citizens.

Thus, the famous Aristotelian proposition that "man is a political animal"–or, more accurately, that "man is by nature an animal intended to live in a polis" (Aristotle 1969, 5)–should be understood as a direct expression of Greek exceptionalism. This proposition was, thus, intended to apply not to all peoples but to the Greeks only.[6] The common interpretation by most scholars that the Aristotelian proposition "man is a political animal" applies to all peoples is an anachronistic misinterpretation. According to Aristotle's teleology, human nature is not common and instinctual to all human beings, but something revealed in the ultimate end (*telos*), as a goal to be attained. In fact, only Greeks, who have reached the stage of living in the polis, are indeed political animals by nature, and barbarians who are "without a polis, by reason of [their] own nature and not of some accident" constitute "a poor sort of being" (Aristotle 1969, 5). According to Aristotle's pristine form of Orientalism, the life of slavery is fit for barbarians when they live in Greece and tyrannical rule is suitable when they live outside it, because they lack reason and the ruling element of free men.

It seems mandatory to examine in more detail the Aristotelian notion of tyranny that is fit for barbarians. For Aristotle, a city-state occupied by free citizens is the ideal political association in which people can pursue their common interest. In contrast, "[t]

6 Doubtless, even Greek women were excluded from its intended application.

hose constitutions which consider only the personal interest of the rulers are all wrong constitutions, or perversions of the right forms" (Aristotle 1969, 112). Furthermore, "[w]e may say that when the One, or the Few, or the Many, rule with a view to the common interest, the constitutions under which they do so must necessarily be right constitutions. On the other hand, the constitutions directed to the personal interest of the One, or the Few, or the Masses, must necessarily be perversions" (Aristotle 1969, 114). Thus, Aristotle presents kingship, aristocracy, and the polity as correct constitutions that pursue the people's common interest, and tyranny, oligarchy, and democracy as perverse. Among the three perversions, tyranny is conceived as the worst form, as it is the perverse form of kingship, the best constitution (Aristotle 1969, 158).

Plato also suggests that tyranny is an extremely corrupt political system. In *The Republic*, he describes the deterioration process of his ideal city and defines *tyranny* as the "extreme illness of a city" (Plato 1968, 222). Likewise, Aristotle also defines *tyranny* as an unnatural state of chaos and confusion: "There is no society which is meant by its nature for rule of the tyrannical type, or for rule of the other types found in wrong or perverted constitutions: the societies that are under such types of rule have fallen into an unnatural condition" (1969, 150). Thus, the supreme duty of citizens is to overcome the unnatural condition of tyranny and restore the natural, normal condition (Aristotle 1969, 150).[7]

For Aristotle, the capacity to overcome tyranny turns out,

7 Hella Mandt is one among contemporary theorists who presents the resistance to tyranny not as a right but as a duty (Mandt 1994, 61).

however, to be a privilege reserved only for "civilized" Greeks. Barbarians, in contrast, are servile and familiar with tyrannical rule and accustomed to living under it. In discussing the natural faculties of citizens fit for his ideal state, Aristotle notes that "[t]he peoples of cold countries generally, and particularly those of Europe, are full of spirit, but deficient in skill and intelligence," and that "[t]he peoples of Asia are endowed with skill and intelligence, but are deficient in spirit." Therefore, Europeans "attain no political development and show no capacity for governing others," and Asians "continue to be peoples of subjects and slaves." In contrast, the Greek stock equipped with the best qualities of the two peoples continues to remain free and is capable of attaining the "highest political development" and "governing every other people–if only it could once achieve political unity" (Aristotle 1969, 296).[8] As these quotes show, Aristotle distinguishes between the Greeks and the Europeans and Asians, calling the latter two barbarian.

Not being satisfied with merely distinguishing between Greeks and barbarians, Aristotle subdivides barbarians even further, presenting Asians as more servile than Europeans: "These uncivilized peoples are more servile in character than Greeks (as the peoples of Asia, in turn, are more servile than those of Europe)" (Aristotle 1969,

8 Thus, according to Ernest Barker, "Aristotle advised Alexander, in the exhortation 'On Colonies,' to distinguish between Greeks and barbarians," treating the former as a constitutional leader and the latter as a despotic master because the latter, including Persians, lacked the capacity to develop virtues. However, Alexander, who had a good sense of balance as a politician, did not follow Aristotle's advice but treated Greeks and Persians equally, promoting "intermarriage and common military service" (Barker 1969, xvii, lix). Thus, Barker continues, "It meant a great revolution," giving birth to "the *cosmopolis* in place and instead of the polis" (Barker 1969, lix).

138). Here, *Asia* refers to the confines of Persia and its vicinities east of the Aegean Sea. Therefore, what Aristotle referred to as Asia included only the ancient "Near East," which was far smaller than what we today understand as Asia (Bae Cheol-hyeon 2001, 205).[9]

Aristotle defines human nature in terms of ethnic differences. He regards Asians as servile, as leading a slavish life without any resistance and taking tyrannical rule for granted. He extends his definition of human nature based on ethnic differences to the political community. Judging from this examination, Aristotle's argument that "[t]here is no society which is meant by its nature for rule of the tyrannical type" (Aristotle 1969, 150) is in fact applicable only to Greek city-states, and tyranny remains natural and constitutional for European and Asian barbarians, as can be seen in the following passage:

> Another type of kingship is the sort which is to be found among some uncivilized [i.e. non-Hellenic] peoples. Kingships of this sort all possess an authority similar to that of tyrannies; but they are, nonetheless, constitutional. . . . The reason is that these uncivilized peoples are more servile in character than Greeks. (Aristotle 1969, 138)

Thus, Aristotle identifies the archetype of tyranny in the Persian monarchy:

9 Due to the constraints of his times, Aristotle could not have extended his research of political systems farther east than Persia.

> Many of its characteristics are supposed to have been originally instituted by Periander of Corinth; but many of its features may also be derived from the Persian system of government. (Aristotle 1969, 244)

From our examination so far, it is evident that the Aristotelian essentialist scheme of civilization-barbarism leads to the conclusion that non-Greek barbarians had neither the capacity nor the right to resist tyranny. Aristotle assumed that barbarians' kingship was permanently tyrannical and impossible to overthrow. In contrast, he supposed that tyrannies in Greece could and should be overturned and that if they did exist in Greece, they were mere perversions.

Aristotle's point might be less disputable had he based his definition of the Persian kingship on empirical research. Clearly, however, Aristotle branded Asia as tyrannical on the basis of his Hellenocentric bias. For him, barbarian tyranny was a natural and normal political system for the servile and slavish Asians, whereas the Greek tyranny was regarded as a temporary and pathological aberration. With this in mind, we will now examine Aristotle's analysis of tyranny in more detail.

Aristotle's Analysis of Tyranny

Aristotle examines and formulates ideal political systems in volumes 2 and 7 of *The Politics* and devotes himself to analyzing actual politics in volumes 3 to 5. He describes and diagnoses tyranny in comparison with other political systems, examines the cause of its collapse, and measures for its preservation in volumes 3 and 4. Aristotle (1969) describes the major features of tyranny thus:

> Tyranny is single-person government of the political association on the line of despotism [i.e., treating the citizens as a master treats slaves]. (Aristotle 1969, 115)
>
> [H]e [the tyrant] too uses coercion by virtue of superior power. (Aristotle 1969, 122)
>
> [T]he tyrant, who rules contrary to the will of his subjects, has a [foreign] bodyguard to protect him against them. (Aristotle 1969, 138)
>
> Tyranny is bound to exist where a single person governs men who are all his peers or superiors, without any form of responsibility, and with a view to his own advantage rather than that of his subjects. (Aristotle 1969, 179)

According to these quotes, Aristotle sees tyranny as a political system that transforms equal relations among free men into those between master and slaves.[10] It also serves the private interest of the ruler, not the common interest of the community. Whereas kingship

10 Here it should be noted that Aristotle investigates tyranny in the Greek polis in which free citizens engage in self-government, whereas tyranny in Persia presupposes unequal relations between men from the beginning.

rules with the consent of subjects and within the legal limit, tyranny neither respects law nor satisfies the consent of subjects as the condition for legitimate political power (Aristotle 1969, 241).[11] If a tyrant feigns taking into consideration the consent of the subjects, he only does so to legitimate his rule for private gains. When he is unable to gain the consent of his subjects, however, he relies upon physical coercion such as foreign bodyguards or mercenaries. He corrupts his citizens and turns them into servile subjects.[12] Thus, tyranny is the most corrupt political regime, an unnatural condition not worthy of being called "political" in the least.

After diagnosing the major symptoms of tyranny, Aristotle examines the causes of its collapse and the necessary measures for its preservation. Its collapse is caused by internal quarrels among partners in a tyranny, the actual attacks of revolutionaries against the office and life of a tyrant, and so on (Aristotle 1969, 237, 240). The reasons why subjects rebel against their tyrants are often "unjust oppression, fear, and contempt" (Aristotle 1969, 237). According to Aristotle, "[t]he honours paid to the man who assassinates a tyrant–and not a mere thief–are also great" (Aristotle 1969, 66).

Aristotle then discusses the method for preserving tyranny. According to him, it is preserved in "two ways which are utterly

---

11 Aristotle asserted that "kingships among uncivilized peoples," for example, in Asia, are thus "of the nature of tyrannies." According to Aristotle, then, the law in the kingships of Asia is a means for maintaining tyranny rather than an instrument for checking it.

12 For example, refer to the following passage: "and when it is imposed, by fraud or by force, it is instantly regarded as a form of tyranny" (Aristotle 1969, 241). In addition, Aristotle's explanation of deceitful actions the tyrant takes to preserve his rule proves this point (Aristotle 1969, 246-50).

opposed to one another." The first is traditional and is "still followed by the majority of tyrants," and the second is the very reverse of the first, "turning of tyranny into the nature of a kingship" (1969, 244, 246). Whereas the first method presupposes that the subjects are hostile to a tyrant and "the aim is to make them unable to conspire," the second aims at "making the subjects indisposed to conspire" (1969, 246n1).

The first method consists of various measures. One is the purge of outstanding and spirited men, as they can be a threat to tyranny. A second is to breed mutual distrust and discord among subjects[13] so that they remain estranged and are unable to launch collective action against their tyrant. A third is to encourage ignorance among subjects and to place all people under the constant surveillance of secret police, thus keeping people in isolation and atomization. A fourth is "impoverishing their subjects," partly to prevent people from having the means for engaging in political action and partly to keep them busy earning a living. Some examples are the waging of frequent wars, imposition of heavy taxes, and initiating large-scale construction works such as the "building of a temple to Olympian Zeus by the family of Peisistratus" (Aristotle 1969, 244-45).

In contrast, the second method seeks to prolong tyranny by disguising it as kingship: "The tyrant should act, or at any rate appear to act, in the role of a good player of the part of King. . . . He should plan and adorn his city as if he were not a tyrant, but a trustee for its benefit. He should always show a particular zeal in the cult of the

13 Thus, we find the following sentence in *The Nicomachean Ethics*: "[Justice] exists least in the worst form: in tyranny there is little or no friendship" (Aristotle 1998, 212).

gods" (Aristotle 1969, 247-48).[14] Just as Glaucon says in Plato's *The Republic* that the "extreme of injustice is to seem to be just when one is not" (Plato 1968, 38), the tyrant, a man of extreme injustice, may prolong his rule by acting as if he were genuinely a just ruler. For example, the tyrant may justify his rule by acting more as a steward than as a tyrant, more as a public arbitrator than as a seeker of private interest, more as a guardian of his subjects than as their dominator, more as people's representative than as their demagogue, and more as a guardian of tradition than as its destroyer. After all, Aristotle ended up bringing the superiority of kingship into sharp relief in his recommendation of the second method (Mandt 1994, 55).

Thus far, we have summarized Aristotle's theory of tyranny. It is interesting to note that the elaborate diagnosis and critique of tyranny was present in classical Confucianism, notably in *The Works of Mencius*, who was Aristotle's contemporary in pre-Qin China. Mencius established the "Theory of the Overthrow and Punishment of a Tyrant" as an important strand in the Confucian tradition, and his theory has laid the groundwork for Confucian justification of revolutionary struggle against tyranny and autocracy. It is mandatory to examine Mencius's theory of tyranny and compare it with Aristotle's.

14 Of course, Aristotle adds the crucial safeguard that "the reformed tyrant shall retain power, and is still in a position to govern his subjects with or without their consent" (Aristotle 1969, 247).

The Theory of the Overthrow and Punishment of Tyrants in Classical Confucianism: The Political Thought of Mencius

Aristotle defines *tyranny* as rule by a single arbitrary ruler and points to Asia (including Persia) as its archetype. However, there is in fact a strong critical voice opposing tyranny in the political thought of Mencius that contradicts Aristotle's Hellenocentric conviction. Mencius's political philosophy may be characterized as the ideal of "kingly rule" (or rule of virtue).[15] Its major features can be summarized as follows: requiring the support and consent of the people as a condition for legitimate political rule; providing basic property (or material needs) for the people; requiring the joint rule of a monarch and ministers to prevent a single, arbitrary rule; abiding by the theory of the overthrow and punishment of tyrants; and, finally, ruling virtuously with generosity (or benevolence) rather than with the strict rule of law with heavy punishment (propagated by Chinese Legalists).

Whereas Aristotle devotes himself considerably to describing major features of tyranny and examining the method for maintaining tyrannical rule, *The Works of Mencius* does not include such considerations. Instead, Mencius focuses his attention mainly on describing major features of genuine kingship, proposing preventive measures against tyranny, and legitimizing the overthrow and

15 A comparison between Confucius and Mencius shows that the latter stressed "righteousness" more strongly than "benevolence" among the Confucian cardinal virtues.

punishment of tyrants.[16] Concrete descriptions of tyranny in Confucian political philosophy can be found mainly in *The Shoo King* (The Book of Historical Documents),[17] as well as in *The Works of Mencius*. We shall next identify major features of tyranny presented in *The Shoo King* and then examine Mencius's critical analysis of tyranny and justification of revolution in comparison with Aristotle's.

The Shoo King and *The Works of Mencius* reflect similarities between Confucian and Aristotelian descriptions of tyranny in the following passages:

> After the death of King Yao and King Shun, the principles that mark sages fell into decay. Oppressive sovereigns arose one after another, who pulled down houses to make ponds and lakes, so that the people could not get clothes and food. Afterwards, corrupt speakings and oppressive deeds became more rife; gardens and parks, ponds and lakes, thickets and marshes

16 This is also the difference between Aristotle and Mencius. Whereas Aristotle examines the method of preserving tyranny as well as overcoming it, Mencius rather takes a firm stand against tyranny. Thus, although both of them display a strong normative attitude in their political analysis, still we could say that Aristotle shows a more positivist temper, whereas Mencius maintains a more normative spirit.

17 *The Shoo King* (Book of Historical Documents: 書經) is a collection of books on history covering the earliest three dynasties in ancient Chinese history. These books were originally kept by the offices of history in various dynasties and were later filed and edited by Confucius. Thus, the theory of the overthrow and punishment of tyrants did not appear first in *The Works of Mencius* but had been present from the beginning of Chinese political thought. However, Confucius did not mention the overthrow and punishment of tyrants in his *Confucian Analects*. Thus, it is Mencius who contributed to promoting the theory into one of the core principles of Confucianism. James Legge translated *Shujing* as *The Shoo King*. Refer to Confucius (1960).

became more numerous, and birds and beasts swarmed. By the time of the tyrant Chau [Zhou], the kingdom was again in a state of great confusion. (Mencius 1960, 280)

The king of Hea [Xia 夏] extinguished his virtue and played the tyrant, extending his oppression over you, the people of the myriad regions. Suffering from his cruel injuries, and unable to endure the wormwood and poison, you protested with one accord your innocence to the spirits of heaven and earth. (Confucius 1960, 186)

Now, Show [Zhou 紂][18] the king of Shang, does not reverence Heaven above, and inflicts calamities on the people below. He has been abandoned to drunkenness, and reckless in lust. He has dared to exercise cruel oppression. Along with criminals he has punished all their relatives. He has put men into office on the hereditary principle. He has made it his pursuit to have palaces, towers, pavilions, embankments, ponds, and all other extravagances, to the most painful injury of you, the myriad people. He has burned and roasted the loyal and good. He has ripped up pregnant women. (Confucius 1960, 284-85)

Now Show [Zhou], the king of Shang treats with contemptuous slight the five constant virtues, and abandons himself to wild idleness and irreverence. He has cut himself off from heaven, and brought enmity between himself and the people. He cut through the leg-bones of those who were wading in the morning; he cut out the heart of the worthy man. By the use of

18 "Show" is the name for Zhou, the last king of Shang.

> his power killing and murdering, he has poisoned and sickened all within the four seas. His honour and confidence are given to the villainous and bad. He has driven from him his instructors and guardians. He has thrown to the winds the statutes and penal laws. He has imprisoned and enslaved the upright officer. He neglects the sacrifices to Heaven and Earth. He has discontinued the offerings in the ancestral temple. He makes contrivances of wonderful device and extraordinary cunning to please his woman. (Confucius 1960, 294-95)

Reading these quotes, it is clear that there are many similarities between Aristotelian and Confucian descriptions of tyranny worthy of close examination. First of all, tyranny in Confucian thought refers to the form of rule enforced entirely by violent and immoral means. As the above quotes show, the foremost feature of tyranny is violent rule of terror that instills constant fear. Such a reign of terror is similar to that of Aristotle's tyrant, who mobilizes coercive force and relies upon foreign bodyguards. It was by ruling with violent and immoral means that Jie and Zhou, the two notorious tyrants, drove people to desert them. Second, just as Aristotle defines *kingship* as rule within the limit of law and *tyranny* as rule in violation of law, the tyrant in *Shujing* is portrayed as an arbitrary destroyer of law, as we can see in the passage, "He has thrown to the winds the statutes and penal laws." Third, Aristotle states that tyranny is maintained by the removal of outstanding men and men of spirit who threaten it, and in *Shujing*, tyrants kill loyal ministers, those representing the will of people, as in the phrase "burning the loyal and the good." Furthermore, "imprison[ing] and enslav[ing] the upright officer" is an idea similar to Aristotle's description of the tyrant who turns free citizens into subjects. Fourth, just as the tyrant in *Shujing* built palaces, towers, pavilions, embankments, ponds, and all other extravagances to increase his own pleasure and to harm his people, so did Aristotle's tyrant impoverish his people by undertaking large-scale construction works. This also confirms Aristotle's point that tyranny is a single person's rule with a view to his own advantage. Finally, Aristotle suggests that the tyrant is a destroyer of tradition by showing that tyrants always need to display particular cultist zeal. Chinese tyrants are also found to destroy tradition, as shown in the passage: "He neglects the sacrifices to Heaven and Earth. He has discontinued offerings in the ancestral temple." Considering all this, it is apparent the discussion of tyranny in classical Confucianism that appears in *The Works of Mencius* and *The Shoo King* is very similar to Aristotle's ideas of tyranny.

Turning to Mencius's critique of tyranny and justification of its overthrow, it should be noted that Mencius stressed the idea of the joint rule of a king and ministers and the will of people as the source of legitimate political rule, either to prevent tyranny or to overthrow it. First of all, it was for the sake of preventing a single man's arbitrary rule that Mencius stressed the joint rule of a king and ministers. King Shun, whom Mencius admired most, was famous for his willingness to consult with and follow others in his rule, instead of insisting on his own way: "He (Shun) regarded virtue as the common property of himself and others, giving up his own way to follow that of others, and delighting to learn from others to practise what was good" (Mencius 1960, 205).

Shun's precedent served as an exemplary model not only for sage kings, but also for kings and lords during the Spring and Autumn period who placed priority on real politics over moral politics:

> There was the behaviour of T'ang [Tang] to I Yin [Li Yin]:– he first learned of him, and then employed him as his minister; and so without difficulty he became kingly sovereign. There was the behaviour of the duke Hwan to Kwan Chung [Guan Zhong]:–he first learned of him, and then employed him as his minister; and so without difficulty he became chief of all the princes. (Mencius 1960, 214)

In Confucian political thought,[19] the relation between king and ministers is basically one of righteousness and reason, so ministers may abandon a king if righteousness and reason are in discord. A king's arbitrary rule over ministers is rejected in Confucian political thought. Furthermore, as is shown in the above quote, Confucianism argues that the king may exercise his rule by learning of his ministers. Mencius warned against the danger of a single rule by a monarch and contributed to consolidating the idea of a joint rule of king and ministers, a uniquely Confucian political idea.

19 How ministers serve the prince depends on how the latter treats the former. "When the prince regards his ministers as his hands and feet, his ministers regard their prince as their belly and heart; when he regards them as the ground or as grass, they regard him as a robber and an enemy" (Mencius 1960, 318). The founder of the Ming empire was allegedly exasperated at this passage and removed it from *The Works of Mencius*, deleting the following passage as well: "The people are the most important element in a nation; the spirits of the land and grain are the next; the sovereign is last" (Mencius 1960, 483). See Huang Zongxi (2000, 54n16).

Mencius also criticized tyrannical rule by employing the analogy of a lapidary. He argued that the government of the country should rely upon expert knowledge and that even a king's authority should not interfere with ministers, just as carving and polishing a gemstone should be completely trusted to a lapidary (Mencius 1960, 168). Mencius's idea of rule by experts is similar to Plato's idea of philosopher-rulers and contrasts sharply with Aristotle's stress on rule by amateurs.

Had Mencius's argument stopped here, then he might have been criticized for merely defending oligarchical rule by a small class of intellectuals or experts, just as Plato has been criticized. However, Mencius was not satisfied with his argument for the joint rule of king and ministers in order to check tyrannical rule. He further proposed the support and consent of the people as the condition for legitimate political power, which may be understood in line with Aristotle's stress on rule with subjects' consent as the essential condition distinguishing kingship from tyranny. The support and consent of the people may be confirmed passively, such as when people welcome a given policy of a king or he makes it a rule to share pleasures with his people. But more important, we find that Mencius insists that power come from the people and be exercised in accordance with their will.

Mencius declares that the source of power lies in the people. According to him, the authority of kings such as Yao and Shun was recognized and given by Heaven, and Heaven in turn also reflected the will of the people. In his explanation of the succession from Yao to Shun, Mencius stated that Heaven and the people respectively accepted Shun when Yao presented Shun to both of them (Mencius

1960, 355). Quoting a passage from *Shujing*, Mencius says that "Heaven sees according as my people see; Heaven hears according as my people hear" (Mencius 1960, 357). This means that Heaven reflects the will of the people, although the two are separate sources of authority.

Regarding the exercise of political power, Mencius explicitly states that the will of the people as a whole should be reflected in important government policies. For example, the appointment of ministers and the penal administration were important government affairs in ancient China, and Mencius stresses that a king should implement such policies as those of appointing and dismissing ministers and passing a death sentence upon a criminal only after all the people approve them. For example, he notes with regard to the appointment of an administrator:

> When all those about you say, "This is a man of talents and worth," you may not therefore believe it. When your great officers all say, "This is a man of talents and virtue," neither may you for that believe it. When all the people say, "This is a man of talents and virtue," then examine the case, and when you find that the man is such, employ him. . . . You must act in this way in order to be the parent of the people. (Mencius 1960, 166)

Mencius asserts here that in appointing ministers, a king should deliberate in a long series of hearing processes with diverse strata of courtiers, ministers, and people, and then make a final decision on the basis of these hearings and his own reflections (Mencius 1960, 166). Mencius places great importance on the will of the people in the policy-making process. Although the mechanism representing the will of the people in ancient Chinese states was not institutionalized, Mencius's political thought clearly incorporates the spirit and idea of representing the will of the people in Confucian political thought. This suggests that Confucian political thought possibly follows the concept "by the people" in addition to the elements "of the people" and "for the people," although it has been commonly thought to contain only the latter two among the three elements of democracy.[20] Mencius's trust in the people's will also indicates that the common argument that Confucian tradition is a critical barrier to the development of democracy in East Asia may be too cursory at best.

Finally, it is important to note that for Mencius, the support and consent of the people is crucial not only in legitimating political power, but also in resisting and overthrowing tyranny. Thus, Mencius stressed the fact that people enthusiastically welcomed kings Tang and Wu as leaders of revolutions when they undertook the overthrow and punishment of tyrants:

> While Tang punished their rulers, he consoled the people. His progress was like the falling of opportune rain, and the people were delighted. It is said in the Book of History [Book of Historical Documents], "We have waited for our prince. When our prince comes, we may escape from the punishment under which we suffer." (Mencius 1960, 273)

20 Of course, this point should not be interpreted as asserting that all Confucian heritage is hospitable to democracy. Rather it only intends to criticize some Western scholars who are more than happy to deny the value of Confucianism due to some of its ostensibly negative aspects.

> Mencius replied, "If the people of Yen [Yan] will be pleased with your taking possession, then do so." Among the ancients there was one who acted on this principle, namely King Wu. "If the people of Yen will not be pleased with your taking possession, then do not do so." Among the ancients there was one who acted on this principle, namely King Wan [Wen]. (Mencius 1960, 273)

People's delight with Tang's "progress" as if it were "the falling of opportune rain" explicitly indicates their active support of and consent to the new political order. Of course, the institutionalized validation procedure of popular support and consent was absent in the times of Mencius. Yet his recognition that political power is effective only when it is based on popular support and consent shows his deep insight into the origin and generation of political power.

In addition, in his legitimization of resistance against tyranny, Mencius argues that the tyrant is not a king but a thief or ruffian:

> The King Hsuan [Xuan 宣] of Chi [Qi 齊] asked, saying, "Was it so, that Tang banished Chieh [Jie], and that King Wu smote Chau [Zhou]?" Mencius replied, "It is so in the records." The king said, "May a minister then put his sovereign to death?" Mencius said, "He who outrages the benevolence proper to his nature is called a robber; he who outrages righteousness is called a ruffian. The robber and ruffian we call a mere fellow. I have heard of the cutting off of the fellow Chau, but I have not heard of the putting a sovereign to death, in his case." (Mencius 1960, 167)

Mencius's calling tyrants "mere fellows" rather than "kings" reverberates in a similar passage in *Two Treatises of Government* by John Locke, who is famous for his theory of resistance. Pointing to the dangerous nature of the arbitrary and tyrannical supreme ruler, Locke states: "But when he quits this Representation, this Public Will, and acts by his own private Will, he degrades himself, and is but a single private Person without Power, and without Will, that has any Right to Obedience" (Locke 1967, 386). Here the "private Person" is equivalent to Mencius's "mere fellow." Mencius's logic of overthrowing and punishing a tyrant is comparable to Aristotle's praise of tyrannicide in which he said that he who kills a tyrant is awarded with great honor. Likewise, Tang and Wu, who overthrew and punished tyrants, have been honored and enshrined as "sage kings" in Confucian political thought.

Mencius's theory and insight, so far delineated, clearly show that Oriental despotism is a Western invention of stigma upon Asia and is inapplicable to ancient Chinese and East Asian civilization and classical Confucianism. Mencius's political philosophy is clearly incompatible with tyranny. Therefore, Mill's derogatory remark that the history of Asia lacks systematic resistance to tyranny is clearly Orientalist ideology based on strong prejudice and poor evidence.

Conclusion

Aristotle defines *tyranny* as a single man's arbitrary rule that is disrespectful of the law, goes against the will of the people, and pursues the ruler's private interest. According to Aristotle, such tyranny seeks to preserve itself by employing various measures such as breeding mutual distrust and fear through constant surveillance, encouraging ignorance and impoverishment of people, and suppressing free political action by citizens. Tyranny thus represents the antithesis of Aristotle's ideal polity, in which governance depends on the support and consent of free citizens and political action is based on deliberative consensus. Aristotle also examines those elements maintaining tyranny and notes that great honors are given to citizens who overthrow tyranny.

Mencius provided a path-breaking turning point in the history of Confucian political thought by elevating the status of people as high as the mandate of Heaven. For Mencius, tyranny, which rules against the will of the people, is the worst political system. The tyrant is no more than a robber or a ruffian who betrays benevolence and righteousness and is thereby demoted to the status of "a mere fellow" who happens to occupy the throne. According to Mencius, tyranny is also an open dictatorship of terror, which fails to provide basic living conditions for people, exercises arbitrary rule of men that trespasses the standard of propriety and law, oppresses virtuous ministers, ignores the popular opinion, and imposes rule by violence. Thus, the tyrant who dominates the people with cruelty and greed rightfully becomes the object of popular grievance and hatred and is a public enemy whose murder will be supported by popular will. For example, when Tang and Wu overthrew and punished Jie and Zhou, they were empowered by popular support and consent. Tang and Wu were able to do it by gaining popular support and consent, whereas Jie and

Zhou were overthrown by losing that support.

Thus far, we have compared Confucian theory of tyranny with that of Aristotle. Through this comparison, we criticized the Aristotelian, Hellenocentric argument that the peoples of Asia were servile and tyranny naturally suited their political system. At the same time, we have found that Aristotelian analysis of tyranny sheds insightful light on understanding tyranny in ancient China and that Mencius's understanding of tyranny was quite similar to that of Aristotle. The political thought of Mencius has remained an important source of East Asian tradition. Mencius encourages and approves of active resistance and struggle against tyranny and oppression and strives for the realization of virtuous "kingly rule." In no way does Mencius preach an "orientalized" tradition that, according to Aristotle and Mill, encourages passivity and discourages resistance against tyrannical rules. Reexamination of political thought in East Asia suggests that traditionally, there was a criteria of judgment for proper politics which asserted that it was legitimate to overthrow and punish tyrants. With this in mind, we will be better equipped to rejuvenate the elements hospitable to progress in East Asian tradition and to conduct a genuine dialogue between Eastern and Western civilizations.

References

English Materials

Aristotle. 1969. *The Politics of Aristotle.* Edited and translated by Ernest Barker. Oxford: Oxford University Press.

——. 1998. *The Nicomachean Ethics.* Translated by David Ross. Oxford: Oxford University Press.

Ashcroft, Bill, Gareth Griffiths, and Helen Tiffin. 1998. *Key Concepts in Post-Colonial Studies.* London: Routledge.

Barker, Ernest. 1969. "Introduction." In Aristotle 1969, xi-lxxvi.

Confucius. 1960. *The Shoo King.* Vol. 3 of *The Chinese Classics*, edited and translated by James Legge. Hong Kong: Hong Kong University Press.

Huntington, Samuel P. 1991. *The Third Wave: Democratization in the Late Twentieth Century.* Norman: University of Oklahoma Press.

Kang, Jung In. 1999. "Confucianism and Democracy in East Asia: A Critique of Samuel P. Huntington's *Third Wave.*" *Korea Journal* 39 (3): 315-37.

——. 2000. "Some Reflections on Recent Democratization in South Korea." *Korea Journal* 40 (2): 195-224.

——. 2003. "The Rule of Law and the Rule of Virtue: On the Necessity for Their Mutual Integration." *Korea Journal* 43 (1): 233-60.

Locke, John. 1967. *Two Treatises of Government*, edited by Peter Laslett. 2nd ed. Cambridge: Cambridge University Press.

Mencius. 1960. *The Works of Mencius.* Vol. 2 of *The Chinese Classics*, edited and translated by James Legge. Hong Kong: Hong Kong

University Press.

Plato. 1968. *The Republic of Plato.* Translated by Allan Bloom. New York: Basic Books.

Richter, Melvin. 1977. *The Political Theory of Montesquieu.* Cambridge: Cambridge University Press.

Korean Materials

Bae, Cheol-hyeon. 2001. "Yureopui Mochereul Chaja" [In Search of the Origin of Europe]. *Gyegan Sasang* [Political Thought Quarterly] 13 (1): 201-21.

Huang, Zongxi. 2000. *Myeongidaebangnok* [Expectation of a New Age]. Translated by Deok-gyun Kim. Seoul: Hangilsa.

Lee, Seung-hwan. 1998. "Seoyangui Yugyo Ihaee Daehan Damnonhakjeok Bunseok" [A Discursive Analysis of Western Understanding of Confucianism]. *Gyegan Sasang* [Political Thought Quarterly] 10 (1): 70-93.

Mandt, Hella. 1994. *Pokjeongnongwa Jeohanggwon* [The Theory of Tyranny and the Right to Resistance]. Translated by Jae-u Sim. Seoul: Minumsa. Originally published as *Tyrannislehre und Widerstandsrecht* (Darmstadt: Luchterhand, 1974).

GLOSSARY

Guan Zhong (Ch.)	管仲	Wen (Ch.)	文
Jie (Ch.)	桀	Wu (Ch.)	武
Mencius (Ch.)	孟子	Xia (Ch.)	夏
Qi (Ch.)	齊	Xuan (Ch.)	宣
Shang (Ch.)	商	Yan (Ch.)	燕
Shujing (Ch.)	書經	Yao (Ch.)	堯

Shun (Ch.)	舜	Yi Yin (Ch.)	伊尹
Tang (Ch.)	湯	Zhou (Ch.)	紂

(Ch. = Chinese)

Chapter 5

On *Datong* (大同) Democracy: A Radical Remembrance of a Lost Tradition?

The purpose of this chapter is to conceptualize primitive democracy glimmering in ancient Confucianism as *Datong* (大同) democracy, explore its vestiges by analyzing and comparing ancient Chinese classical–Confucian and historical–texts, and then trace its radical remembrance by East Asian Confucian intellectuals in the nineteenth century. To fulfill this purpose, first, I review existing literature in ancient history to show that the concept of democracy or a republic was not confined to areas in the Mediterranean, such as ancient Greece and Rome, but was widely observed in ancient Mesopotamian civilizations. This is intended to liberate our imagination from the commonly held notion that the concept of democracy or a republic was only a Western invention and to prepare us to find a similar kind of polity in other ancient civilizations, notably East Asia. Second, I suggest that the concept of *Datong* has two meanings, "great harmony" and "great consensus," and that what I mean by *Datong* democracy is "democracy by great consensus." Third, I present the political decisions surrounding the abdication of the throne (*chanrang* 禪讓) by such legendary sage kings as Yao (堯), Shun (舜), and Yu (禹) as the prototype of *Datong* democracy and compare Confucius and Mencius in this regard to show that the latter was more democratic than the former. Finally, I show that *Datong* democracy was radically recollected by nineteenth-century East Asian intellectuals who struggled to meet the challenge posed by the incoming Western civilization. For this purpose, political thoughts of Jeong Yakyong (1762-1836) in Korea, Yokoi Shonan (横井小楠, 1809-69) in Japan, and Liang Qi-chao (梁啓超, 1873-1929) are briefly reviewed.[1]

Introduction

The dichotomy of "Western Republicanism versus the Oriental Prince" or "Western Freedom versus Oriental Despotism," as a political symbol, has been a popular subject of preoccupation for modern Western countries for a long time and, simultaneously, a familiar stereotype taken for granted even by non-Western nations. The Athenian democracy of ancient Greece has typically been placed at

1 As I shall discuss later in the chapter, when Yokoi Shonan and Liang Qi-chao radically recollected Yao-Shun's reign as *Datong* democracy, it is clear that they did so deeply impressed by American democracy with its presidential system. It is intriguing, however, to observe that Jeong Yakyong engaged in radical recollection in the early nineteenth century without any clear Western influence identified.

the center of such widespread beliefs. For example, Moses I. Finley, an eminent historian of ancient Greek civilization, has stressed the unique status of the city-states in ancient Greek and Roman civilizations:

> However, all the city-states had in common one feature, the incorporation of peasants, craftsmen and shopkeepers into the political community as members, as citizens; even those who had neither the obligation nor the privilege of bearing arms, it is important to underscore. They were not at first (and in some communities never) members with full rights, not citizens in the full sense that the term acquired in classical Greece and Rome. But even limited recognition was without precedent in history. . . . Any account of Greek or Roman politics must properly acknowledge that radical socio-political innovation. (Finley 1983, 15)

In another passage, Finley also asserts: "The Greeks, and only the Greeks, discovered democracy in that sense, precisely as Christopher Columbus, not some Viking seaman, discovered America" (Finley 1973, 14).

However, ample evidence now accumulated in the fields of archaeology, epigraphy, and comparative history suggests that political entities similar to ancient Athenian democracy or the Roman republic existed throughout the wider Mediterranean and the Orient and had done so much earlier there than in ancient Greece or Rome. Patricia Springborg argues that "the ancient Middle East may well have pioneered city-republican forms, of which the Greek polis was only an example" (Springborg 1992, 3; cf. Vlassopoulos 2007, 102). Thus, contrary to the commonly held Eurocentric historiography that treats ancient Greek history as part of Western or European history, the opposing argument that it should be treated as part of the history of the wider Mediterranean and the Oriental world has been raised and has now secured wide currency. According to this view, the democratic or republican form of government in a city-state was not found only in ancient Greece and Rome but was widely observed in the Oriental world as well. The fact that ancient Athens has monopolized the glory as the birthplace of democracy is only due to modern Eurocentric historiography, which is nothing more than historical myopia.

Considering the significant implications of this revisionist study in comparative history, it seems interesting to ask whether a democratic or republican form of government might have existed in the city-states of ancient China, one of the four cradles of ancient civilization–before the rise and consolidation of a centralized dynastic kingdom–as part of the universal phenomena in the ancient world, though its form and content might have differed from those found in ancient Greece or other parts of the Oriental world. In order to answer this question, this chapter explores the ideation of primitive democracy in ancient Chinese classical literature such as Confucian texts and historiography, with the hope that historians and archaeologists will be motivated to carry out a similar task by attempting to excavate the historical remains of ancient Chinese civilization.

To do this, I set the definition of *democracy* as "rule by the people," being faithful to its original concept, and determine the existence of democracy according to whether ordinary people participated widely in important political decisions such as electing supreme political leaders, appointing and dismissing public officers, and making laws. Bearing in mind the characteristics of ancient societies where kings and nobles (or elders) existed widely, however, I extend the concept of democracy to incorporate a republican form of government for the sake of analytic convenience.[2] As a result of my initial investigation of Chinese classical works, it seems possible to identify the idea of primitive democracy, which I conceptualize as *Datong* (大同) democracy and elaborate on it in this chapter by focusing on the concept of *Datong*, which appeared in *The Shoo King* [書經] or *The Book of Historical Documents* (hereafter, BHD).

However, the vestiges were scattered in the literature, often in the form of inchoate fragments and hidden pictures submerged in the vast sea of anti- or nondemocratic passages. It therefore became necessary to search for latent information in order to discern various democratic fragments scattered throughout the vast literature and weave them into a picture of democracy in an imaginative way. Although it is not conclusive, a preliminary overview of the result of the initial analysis will be presented here to stimulate further research.

Bearing this purpose in mind, this chapter proceeds in the following order. First, based on the cumulative outcome of the research on Western scholarship, an examination is conducted into the extent of the democracy existing in the ancient world and the uniqueness of Athenian democracy in the history of ancient democracies. This

2 According to my extended conception of democracy, the Athenian democracy in its heyday (which effectively reduced the power of aristocratic/oligarchic elements) should be considered a specific form of democracy that realized rule by the people to the fullest possible degree. In addition, my conception includes a wide variety of the republican form of government as democracy, as long as it guarantees substantial participation of the popular sector. Thus, it would include a democratic republic but not an aristocratic one.

examination is necessary, first, to prepare the ground for articulating the ideation of a democratic form of polity in ancient Chinese civilization; no one has ever presented substantial argument and convincing evidence to support claims of the existence of such a body. For example, Confucianism has been credited for two of the elements of democracy, "of the people" (*minben* 民本) and "for the people" (*weimin* 爲民), but never for "by the people" (*minzhu* 民主). Thus, it seems necessary to show that a democratic form of government existed widely in ancient civilizations in the Mediterranean and Mesopotamian world and to take advantage of such historical facts to give credence to my novel presumption that such a form of government had also existed in ancient Chinese civilization. Second, it is necessary to overcome the mainstream academic tendency to determine the existence of democracy in ancient civilizations according to the model of Athenian democracy. However, it should be noted that the achievement of Athenian democracy is unique and exceptional in the sense that it was the outcome of an unusual combination of a "historical backwardness," whereby Greek civilization was not able to establish an ancient empire with a centralized authority like that of Persia and Assyria, and the "belated overripe-ness" of democracy, which was made possible by the unusual prolongation of city-states and consequent prosperity of democracy financed by the imperial status of Athens. Thus, though we have to acknowledge the unique and unprecedented achievement of Athenian democracy in the history of democracy, for this very uniqueness we cannot take the Athenian version as the standard model by which to determine the existence and extent of democracy in other ancient civilizations. Thus, when we accept the possibly (relatively) widespread existence of democracy in the ancient world and the unique status of Athenian democracy, which disqualifies it as the touchstone of democracy, we may be able to open a theoretical space for examining the previously unacknowledged existence of democracy in ancient Chinese civilization.

Second, in order to advance the concept of *Datong* democracy, two concepts of *Datong* will be identified and clarified in the Confucian texts: one as "great harmony" and the other as "great consensus" (or "great concord"). In addition, *Datong* democracy is articulated by relying upon the second concept, and thus *Datong* democracy is defined as "democracy by great consensus."

Third, based on this clarification, the decision-making process involved in the transfer of the throne between Yao (堯), Shun (舜), and Yu (禹)—perhaps including Qi (啓), albeit debatable, as examined later—which is described with rich elaboration and analysis in *The Works of Mencius* (孟子; hereafter, *WM*) and appears later in *The Grand Scribe's Records* (Shi Ji 史記; hereafter, *GSR*) compiled two thousand years ago by the great Chinese historian Ssu-ma Ch'ien [Sima Qian 司馬遷, c. 145-86 BCE] , will be conceptualized as the prototype of *Datong* democracy. Then it will be shown that Mencius is more in favor of *Datong* democracy than Confucius by the comparative analysis of their political thought.

In addition, it will be shown that the vestiges of *Datong* democracy were radically retrieved in the two fragments written by Jeong Yakyong (丁若鏞, 1762-1836), one of the greatest Confucian thinkers of the Joseon dynasty of Korea in the late eighteenth and early nineteenth centuries; that is, "On the Origin of Ministers" (Wonmok 原牧) and "Discussing Tang" (Tangron 湯論). It is interesting to note that Jeong's fragments do not show any visible Western influence, whereas Yokoi Shonan (横井小楠, 1809-69) and Liang Qi-chao (梁啓超, 1873-1929) were clearly aware of Western democracies. Many scholars may wonder why Jeong's two fragments are to be examined. In response to this, it seems important to recognize the possibility that major texts analyzed in this chapter, such as *BHD* (*The Shoo King* 書經), *The Confucian Analects* (Lunyu 論語; hereafter, *CA*), *WM*, and *GSR*, were not completed by the particular disciples of Confucius and Mencius or even by Sima Qian himself, but rather were canonized in the continual and cumulative process of selection and compilation in which the concentration of power into an absolute emperor was legitimized and the vestiges and records of *Datong* democracy were deliberately destroyed and erased in the early Han (漢) empire. Nevertheless, *WM*, for some reason, was able to preserve the memory of *Datong* democracy with unusual vividness and vibrant vigor, which therefore justifies serious examination. However, even though Confucian texts had been established as the sacred canons that legitimized the absolute authority of the emperor and at the same time had been used as official textbooks for education since the Han empire, the memory and record of *Datong* democracy has become almost extinct. As a result, even Huang Zongxi (黃宗羲, 1610-95), a famous Confucian thinker called the "Chinese Rousseau," who lived in the transition period from the Ming (明) to the Qing (淸) empire, once made a bold argument that "the people are the host, while a monarch is only a guest" (Huang Zhongxi 2000, 51), but he failed to present any viable argument to substantiate any notion of democracy. In contrast, Jeong Yakyong confirmed that the people are the subject of politics and declared the principle of *Datong* democracy in selecting political leaders and making laws. In this sense, he resurrected *Datong* democracy with radical remembrance in a form that has preserved its archetype intact and glimmering across more than two thousand years since Mencius. In conclusion, finally, I shall describe the limitations inherent in this preliminary attempt to articulate the idea of *Datong* democracy without presenting any institutional infrastructure for it so as to stimulate further research in the future.

Democracy in the Ancient World: Athenian Democracy Is Unique but Not Alone

Relatively Widespread Existence of Democracy in the Ancient World

Inventing and innovating democracy to the greatest possible extent, ancient Athens made an immense contribution to the history of democracy, not to mention its other more valuable contributions. Thus, Athenian democracy has been accepted as the cradle of democracy, serving as the universal political ideal in the contemporary world. Modern Europeans formulated the dichotomy of "Western freedom versus Oriental despotism" in their process of appropriating ancient Athenian democracy, following the Greek "prejudice," especially drawing upon the heritage left by Aristotle's *Politics*. It was a recycling of "Greek freedom versus Persian (or Asian) tyranny," which the Greeks developed against Persia during the Greco-Persian Wars. However, this dichotomy advanced by the ancient Greeks and modern Europeans has been widely criticized as unfounded in recent comparative historical studies of the ancient civilizations and so has become regarded as the product of Hellenocentrism and Orientalism/Eurocentrism (Wolff 1982; Bernal 1987; Springborg 1992; Vlassopoulos 2007). Considering that the purpose of this chapter is to seek the vestiges of the ideation of democracy glimmering in ancient Chinese political thought, one of the most notable achievements in this revisionist research is the discovery that some form of primitive democracy existed widely in the ancient world. According to Springborg's aforementioned argument that the Greek polis was merely an example of the city-republican forms pioneered by the ancient Orient, ancient Greek civilization did not exist as an exceptional civilization in isolation but as an integral part of the much greater Mesopotamian and Mediterranean civilizations. These ancient civilizations arose due to the prosperity of cities, and the development of democratic politics was also made possible by the growth of free cities in which commerce and trade could prosper. The growth of cities was the cumulative outcome of the dense social interaction of equals coming together to exchange commodities for the mutual satisfaction of their needs. Preconditions for this social intercourse were the laws of private property and contract and commercial laws, with which ancient city-states in Mesopotamia were fully equipped. This prosperous urban life established the basis of wider participation in the power and communal autonomy that constituted politics as a form of close interaction among citizens, which was peculiar to the polis (Springborg 1992, 3, 10).[3]

3 Numerous walled cities–that is, *guo* (國)–had existed as independent agrarian city-states since Xia (夏), Yin (殷), and Zhou (周) in ancient China. Their number was drastically reduced during the Spring and Autumn and Warring

Kostas Vlassopoulos's examination revealed a clear distinction between free citizens and slaves and that "citizenship, self-government and identification with a polis were common property" (2007, 104) in many parts of the ancient Orient, notably in Mesopotamia. Springborg identifies the important components of the city-republican forms in the ancient Orient more concretely:

> These comprise the bicameral legislature, eligibility to which was decided on property qualifications and birth to free citizens; rule of law, an independent judiciary, procedures for holding magistrates to account and trial by jury; the rotation of magistracies among an isonomous elite; voting by ballot and by lot; private laws of contract and commercial law. (Springborg 1992, 3)

Springborg also illustrates her argument with specific examples:

> From c. 1894-1595 BC evidence exists for a bicameral assembly in Sippar [of Sumer], the upper house of which was controlled by the nobility, the lower house confined to commoners, access being granted on property qualifications. Magistracies, appointed on an annual basis, were rotated among an isonomous elite constituted by the judicial, administrative and merchant classes. (Springborg 1992, 8)

State periods (770-221 BCE), which should be seen as the period of hegemonic struggles among city-states that prepared the transition to a centralized empire such as Qin (秦) and Han (漢). It is worth noting the Chinese character *guo* now refers to the state.

The continual existence of self-governing city-states in the ancient Orient seems to contradict the strong presence and expansion of such great empires as Babylonia and, subsequently, Assyria. Many city-states under the reign of Babylonia and Assyria, however, enjoyed great autonomy. For example, there was no overall political identity covering the unified kingdom of Babylonia in which the political identification was given only to the name of the cities and the king was simply "the king of Babylon," the capital city of the loose empire. Thus, a subject of the king of Babylonia was always a citizen of a city (or a member of a tribal group), never a citizen of Babylonia, enjoying the privileges accompanying city-states (Vlassopoulos 2007, 107). This suggests that the international order then prevailing in this region was overlapping, multilayered, and fluid, so that the king who unified this area had to concede wide autonomy and privileges to maintain and foster alliance with many cities. The residents of a city were allowed a large degree of independence, especially exempted from "royal taxation, corvée and military duties." Such freedom was referred to as *kidinnu* in the Akkadian word, a "divinely enforced security" (Vlassopoulos 2007, 107).

This situation, under which city-states were subjugated by the strong kingdom but which allowed them to entertain a high level of republican autonomy, suggests that ancient kingdoms were not able to develop high-level administrative capacity including the bureaucracy to execute a strongly centralized authority. With the emergence of the neo-Babylonian and the Persian kingdoms, however, the changing geopolitical situations began to pose a threat to the republican autonomy of cities. Instead of maintaining Babylonian cities as allies,

Persian kings now incorporated them into their territory to rule them directly (Vlassopoulos 2007, 108). Thus, through a series of complicated developments accompanying the "capacity of irrigation societies," ancient Sumeria, Mesopotamia, Egypt, and China were able to make the decisive transition from city-states to empires with a highly centralized authority (Springborg 1992, 7). Springborg notes the following developmental capacities to make the transition possible:

> (a) impersonal government administered by a bureaucracy; (b) the conception of man as citizen; (c) forms of political representation; (d) the creation of an economic surplus; (e) a monetarized economy, accompanied by the institutions of credit, commercial law, trade treaties and international laws of contract; (f) a standing army, equipped with advanced military technologies; (g) social stratification along functional lines, comprising classes of farmers, artisans, merchants, an administrative elite and priestly caste; (h) the concept of nature as governed by rational laws; (i) institutions for the acquisition, organization and dissemination of knowledge; (j) the development of writing and basic sciences of mathematics, geometry, astronomy, navigation, architecture, engineering and highly developed skills in construction, metal-working, pottery, textiles, sculpture and painting. (Springborg 1992, 7)

In contrast to these ancient empires, Athens and other Greek poleis had not been able to make such a transition due to their failure to develop these capacities; they were finally subjugated by Macedonia and fell into ultimate decline. When ancient Greek poleis experienced population increase and found themselves unable to shoulder it politically and administratively, they had to send part of their population abroad to build new colonies. This fact also suggests the political immaturity of the Greek polis. In other words, it indicates the relative backwardness of Greek politics in contrast to the political capacity found in Egypt and the Orient, in which great empires had been developed to rule over a vast territory and a large population with a centralized authority. But although ancient Greek civilization was considered backward in terms of its capacity to build and consolidate an empire, Athenian democracy was able to make an unprecedented contribution to the rich historical records in its experiment with democracy and profound theoretical insights–represented by Thucydides, Plato, Aristotle, and so on–into it by virtue of Athens's unusual longevity and prosperity, to which we now turn.

The Uniqueness of Athenian Democracy

Athenian democracy was initiated by Solon's reform in 594 BCE and was established fully in about 500 BCE by Cleisthenes's radical reform. Athens was then able to rise up to consolidate its hegemonic power in Greece following a series of events such as its decisive contribution to the victorious defense of Greece in the Greco-Persian Wars, the transfer of the headquarters of the Delian League from Delos to Athens in 454 BCE, and a leading role in concluding the Peace of Kallias with Persia in 448 BCE. Athenian democracy also reached its climax with the reign of Pericles. However, Athenian democracy fell into disgrace with the defeat in the Peloponnesian War in 404 BCE and was vanquished by the conquest of Macedonia in 338 BCE.

Here it is worth noting that the rise and fall of Athenian

democracy coincided with those of the Persian empire (550-330 BCE), which harassed and invaded Greece many times. During this period, although Greek poleis were not able to make a transition to a great empire like Persia, they were able to maintain and prolong their government as city-states–which had already been demolished in Lydia, Cardia, and Egypt by the conquest of Persia–and develop their full potential. An additional aspect of the constitutional form of Greek poleis, as Vlassopoulos points out, is that oligarchies of various sorts did constitute the mainstream of Greek political experience, and democracy was only a variant among the wider subject of ancient Greek poleis constitutions (Vlassopoulos 2007, 116). Furthermore, as a notable and sophisticated example, the Athenian form of democracy was made possible only by the city's assumption of imperial status in Greece. That is, the strength of Athenian democracy depended largely on its imperial status within the Greek political world-system, which permitted complete sovereignty in a modern understanding without succumbing to outside interference and subordination and financed the extension of citizenship to lower classes with material wealth, including copious tributes collected from other Greek poleis. By virtue of this advantage, Athens was able to develop democracy to the greatest possible extent and prolong it far longer than other Greek poleis and other republican city-states in the Orient.

In addition, whereas self-governing and republican city-states in the Orient were not able to leave a systematic record of their democracy, Athens, which was a latecomer to the experiment with democracy but prolonged it to a later period, accumulated theoretical insight into democracy on the basis of this prolonged experience and enjoyed the advantage of using parchment to make a durable record of democracy. These advantages were unavailable to Mesopotamian republics before the first millennium BCE, which could leave only inscriptions on hard materials including clay tablets. In this sense, Aristotle's *Politics,* which contained ample facts about Athenian democracy and theoretical insight into it, maintains an exceptional and outstanding status. Therefore, there is no denying that Athenian democracy has left an immortal historical and theoretical legacy of great contributions to the world history of democracy. However, it is one thing to acknowledge this great achievement of Athenian democracy, but another to deny the historical fact that democracy in the city-states was dispersed widely in other ancient civilizations, including the Orient, and not just in ancient Greece.

The Two Concepts of *Datong: The Book of Rituals and The Book of Historical Documents*

We can find and confirm the two important concepts of *Datong* in ancient Confucian texts. The first is the well-known portrayal of the Confucian ideal society that is described together with *Xiaokang* (小康: Little Prosperity) in *The Book of Rituals* (*Liji* 禮記; hereafter *BR*), and the other is the one that presents the decision-making process of sage kings in *BHD*. Whereas many scholars have historically focused on the former concept of *Datong* together with *Xiaokang* as the Confucian ideal society, the latter has received hardly any attention among Confucian scholars in China, Korea, and Japan. For example,

Zhuxi (朱熹), the foremost neo-Confucian in the Song (宋) dynasty, who innovated and synthesized Confucianism to a new level, digesting the influence of Taoism and Buddhism then prevailing, hardly paid any attention to *Datong* as a decision-making process at all. It is indeed a baffling paradox to note that Zhuxi, despite his stature, never focused on *Datong*, and all the more so to observe that Confucian scholars have never related "*Datong* as the ideal society" to "*Datong* as the decision-making process" of sage kings in the history of Confucianism, as I shall elaborate later. Thus, I want to present the two concepts of *Datong* drawn from Confucian texts, suggest my interpretation that *Datong* as a decision-making process is the prototype of a Confucian version of a primitive democracy, and trace the trajectory of *Datong* democracy glimmering in the history of ancient Confucianism.

Datong Portrayed in *The Book of Rituals*

Datong is described in BR by Confucius as follows:

> When the great way prevailed, all-under-the-heaven was for the public. Those with wisdom and ability were nominated and elected to teach trust and cultivate amicable harmony. As a result, people were not only kind and respectful to their own parents [but also to others' parents], not only taking care of their own children [but also others' children]. The old would enjoy their remaining years comfortably. The young would be put to use to demonstrate their own abilities, and the children would be protected for their well-being and growth. The widows, the widowers, the orphans, old folks without children, and those stricken with illness would all be provided

> for. Males would have their suitable occupations, and females their marriage and home. It was regrettable that resources were wasted, but they were not hoarded only for an individual's use. It is regrettable that one does not exert oneself, but one works not necessarily just for one's benefit. Thus cunning schemes did never occur, nor did thefts and rebellions. People did not have to lock the outside door to their home. This is called *Datong* [the Great Harmony].[4]

Confucianism has believed that the above-quoted *Datong* society, "all-under-the-heaven for the public" existed historically with *Xiaokang* (小康) society, "all-under-the-heaven for the family." Thus, the legendary era reigned by the sage kings Yao (堯) and Shun (舜) is called *Datong* society, whereas the period when Yu (禹; the first king of the Xia [夏] dynasty), Tang (湯; the first king of the Shang [商] dynasty), King Wen (文), King Wu (武), King Cheng (成), and the Duke and Regent of Zhou (周公) ruled is described as the *Xiaokang* society. Here in *Datong* society, all-under-the-heaven belonged to and existed for the public, which indicates in particular the voluntary abdication and transfer of the throne to the wise and virtuous instead of hereditary transfer. Individual virtue and talent were respected, and universal human love beyond the distinction between the self and others prevailed. Moreover, attachment to private property (for personal use) was rather weak, if any notion of private property existed at all; social welfare in the contemporary sense was fully provided for; and as there were no oppressed classes or

4 The concept of *Xiaokang* (小康) is not examined here, as it is not directly related to the purpose of this chapter.

strata, internal and external peace was fully realized without any social conflicts, crimes, or wars. Thus, as there was no need to mobilize or exert physical coercion, political power was exercised with full public spirit and without any private purpose, so that its major function was confined to educating and cultivating people by appointing the wise and capable and building trust and harmony. In this way, *Datong* society was a harmonious society centered on moral rule and enduring peace among people. In this sense, *Datong* described in *BR* may be characterized as the society of "great harmony." However, not a few Confucian scholars have suspected with plausible reasons that the portrayal of *Datong* and *Xiaokang* in *BR* was an insertion by later scholars rather than a direct remark by Confucius. Nevertheless, respecting the long influence exerted upon Confucianism by the portrayal of *Datong*, the prevailing interpretation still holds that *Datong* is the ultimate ideal of Confucianism, whereas *Xiaokang* is the ideal realizable in actual society where a distinction exists between the self and others.

Datong Presented in *The Book of Historical Documents*

Although the reign of the kings Yao and Shun is commonly regarded as a *Datong* society in the Confucian tradition, no direct reference to *Datong* designating Yao-Shun's reign appears in *BHD* or *GSR* (*Shih chi* 史記; the first and greatest book of China's two-thousand-year-old history), both of which contain rich records of Yao-Shun's reign. Furthermore, Yao-Shun's reign as described in *BHD* is actually much closer to *Xiaokang* than to *Datong*, except for the voluntary abdication and transfer of the throne among the sage kings of Yao, Shun, and Yu, which is, as a matter of fact, the most notable indicator characterizing *Datong* society.[5] In this context, the way that Mencius vividly describes the transfer of the throne from Yao to Shun and then from Shun to Yu is significant, corresponding exactly to the second concept of *Datong*, which is presented as a political decision-making process in *BHD*. In this regard, the voluntary abdication of the throne characteristic of the *Datong* society fits closely with *Datong* as a decision-making process. This point has never been fully examined by Confucian scholars, and the focus of this chapter is to elaborate it in a new light.

In *BHD*, the word *Datong* appeared only once. According to the description there, after defeating and overthrowing the Shang (商) dynasty, King Wu (武) paid a visit to the viscount of Ji (箕子) and inquired of him the constitution that Heaven had given to humankind in order to aid the harmonious development in their various conditions, saying, "I do not know how their proper virtues in their various relations should be brought forth in due order" (Great Plan, Book of Zhou; *BHD*, 320). Then the viscount of Ji gave full explanation of the "Great Plan with Its Nine Divisions," which Heaven once revealed to King Yu (the first king of Xia) in order to bring forth the proper virtues of the various relations in their order (*BHD*, 323). In the seventh division, Ji mentioned *Datong* in the following:

> If you have doubts about any great matter, consult with your own heart; consult with your nobles and officers; consult with

5 I do not elaborate this point, as it is not directly related to the theme of this chapter.

> the masses of the people; consult the tortoise and milfoil. If you, the tortoise, the milfoil, the nobles and officers, and the common people all consent to a course, this is what is called a great concord [*Datong*], and the result will be the welfare of your person and good fortune to your descendants. (Great Plan, Book of Zhou; *BHD*, 337)

Here it is worth noting that the Great Plan the viscount of Ji transmitted to King Wu should be regarded as the constitutional norms and fundamental values that had been handed down successively to Confucian kings and thereby internalized earnestly among them, regardless of whether they were put into practice in reality, as *BHD* had long been an essential text for educating Confucian rulers. Thus, I want to interpret *Datong* mentioned in the Great Plan as a mode of decision-making through "Great Consensus" (or "Great Concord"), in contrast to *Datong* in *BR* as "Great Harmony." *Datong* as Great Consensus imparts strong democratic significance because it was a mode of decision-making arrived at by the overlapping consensus among the king, nobles and officers, and the masses of the people as well as the divination sign.[6] Thus, I call

6 Here an objection might be raised that if the authority to make a final decision still belongs to a king, although the opinions of nobles and masses are consulted and respected, then the seventh division would not validate my theory of *Datong* democracy. With regard to this critique, two points can be offered. One is that my concept of *Datong* democracy is flexible enough to include a republican form of government, as I point out in the beginning of this chapter. If the final decision-making authority belongs to either a king or nobles in a republic, then it is an aristocratic republic, falling short of a popular republic, as the historical forms of republican polity are diverse. The other point to make is that we should note several paragraphs (i.e., 27-29) in the seventh division of the Great Plan that may be basically summarized to state

this decision-making "*Datong* democracy."

In order to avoid potential misunderstanding among readers who are familiar with *Datong*, the Confucian ideal society, I need to stress that the main purpose of this chapter is not *Datong* as the ideal society but *Datong* as a mode of democratic decision-making that has long been neglected or buried in oblivion by most Confucian scholars. Once *Datong* democracy is conceptualized in this way, the question naturally arises as to whether we can find any concrete examples of it, either textual or historical, in which democracy is considered, by strong consensus, to have been put into practice. Yet, as it does not seem easy to find any examples that would substantiate *Datong* democracy by great consensus, we may suspect that it is merely a proclamatory and abstract rhetoric rather than a constitutional norm or a fundamental value. Is this presumption correct?

Datong Democracy Glimmering in Ancient Confucianism

In this section, the vestige of the ideation of *Datong* democracy is traced in Confucian texts and the historiography of ancient China. This task necessitates the assembling of a complicated jigsaw and

that if the tortoise, the milfoil, and one of the three political parties among a king, nobles, and the commoners agree even though the other two parties disagree, the result will be still fortunate (Great Plan, Book of Zhou; *BHD*, 337-38). Thus, these paragraphs show that the three parties are formally equal in decision-making and none of the three has the final say in making decisions, as far as the literary description goes.

the searching for hidden pictures to fill in the blanks by comparing Confucian classics and historiography that deal with the same historical periods, figures, and events. To do this, I analyze the process of a series of successions of the throne from Yao (堯), Shun (舜), and Yu (禹) to Shun, Yu, and Qi (啓), respectively, relying mainly upon *WM*, and show that they fit exactly into the *Datong* democracy suggested in the Great Plan. Then I contrast the negative attitude of Confucius toward democracy with the positive one of Mencius, first by noting Confucius's glaring quiescence about *Datong* democracy in the transfer of the throne among Yao (堯), Shun (舜), Yu (禹), and Qi (啓) in contrast to Mencius's vivid account of it. In addition, I pay special attention to the silence of Confucius about the principle of *Datong* democracy by omitting the remonstrance of the Duke of Zhao (召). The Duke of Zhao in Zhou (周) once made a strong remonstrance to King Li (厲), protesting his despotic rule and reminding him of the principle of *Datong* democracy. It is fascinating, however, to note that the remonstrance is omitted in *BHD* compiled by Confucius, whereas it is vividly preserved in *GSR* (*Shi Ji* 史記) and *Guo Yu* (國語), a book of Chinese history compiled in the early Warring States period.

Datong Democracy in the Voluntary Transfer of the Throne among Yao, Shun, and Yu

Above all else, we may find the cases that show *Datong* democracy in Mencius's detailed account of the abdication of thrones by Yao, Shun, and Yu and their consequent succession. Mencius conducts an elaborate analysis of a series of complicated royal successions in part 1 of Wanzhang (萬章) in *WM* in which Yao (堯) and Shun (舜) set up

Shun and Yu (禹), respectively, as regent. In both cases, the latter took the throne after the demise of the former; whereas, Yu's son Qi (啓) took the throne instead of Yi (益), so the process ended up becoming the hereditary succession when Yu passed away, even though Yu had set up Yi as the regent. According to Mencius's interpretation, the sons of Yao and Shun were unworthy, but Shun and Yu were wise and served as regent, conferring benefits on the people for a long time, so they succeeded to the throne after the deaths of Yao and Shun, respectively. The situation is different in the case of Yu. Whereas Yu presented Yi to Heaven and Yi had served only seven years when Yu died, Qi, the son of Yu, was able, as a man of talents and virtue, so the people followed Qi instead of Yi after the death of Yu and he reverently took the throne. Thus, Mencius concludes that the succession was determined by the periods of service of Shun, Yu, and Yi and the worthiness of the sons of Yao, Shun, and Yu (*WM*, 359).

Considering all this together, it seems that the (automatic) succession of the worthiest to the throne was not the general norm even during the reign of Yao and Shun, known as the era of *Datong*. Rather, it seems that the succession was determined by the competitive choice that princes, ministers, and the people made between the son of the sovereign and the regent the preceding sovereign had presented to Heaven. Mencius interprets the outcome of such choice as the will of heaven (*WM*, 358). Thus, on Mencius's explanation it seems possible to infer that princes, ministers, and the people might have chosen and followed the sons of Yao and Shun if the sons had been worthy and the length of time that Shun and Yu served the government had been shorter. However, because the sons of Yao and Shun were not worthy and the periods of service rendered by Shun and Yu were longer, Shun and Yu were chosen for the throne.

It is intriguing, here, to note that the sons of the sovereign were privileged over the worthiest in succession on three points. First, the sovereign's son may inherit the throne if he is able to take care of the achievement of the preceding sovereign (his father), even though he is not equal to the worthiest. Second, to be selected as the sovereign, the worthiest had to be presented as regent to Heaven by the sovereign and had to confer benefits on the people for a long time, whereas the son did not have to acquire such recommendation or shoulder such a burden of long public service. Thus, Mencius said, "In the case of a private individual obtaining the throne, there must be in him virtue equal to that of Shun or Yu; and moreover there must be the presenting of him to Heaven by the preceding sovereign" (*WM*, 359-60). Third, Shun, Yu, and Yi had to go to a remote place, withdrawing themselves from the son of the preceding sovereign when the three years' mourning had expired after the death of the preceding sovereign, so the son might be chosen with ease by princes, nobles, ministers, and the people. In contrast, the unworthy sons of Yao and Shun as well as the virtuous Qi, the son of Yu, did not have to hide themselves. Considering all this privilege enjoyed by the sons of the sovereign, we may argue that the principle of "all-under-the-heaven for the public," one of the notable characteristics of the *Datong* society, was not fully respected even during the reign of Yao and Shun in the sense that the throne ("all-under-the-heaven") was open to the worthiest equally.

Returning to the theme of *Datong* democracy, it is fascinating to find a concrete example of *Datong* democracy by great consensus in Mencius's explanation of the competitive choice between the worthiest and the son of the preceding sovereign as the next sovereign. As a matter of fact, the next sovereign was elected on the recommendation of the preceding sovereign to Heaven, the consent of the princes and ministers, and the support of the people (i.e., a kind of overlapping consensus among the major interested parties); that is, *Datong* democracy. By stating that "The sovereign cannot give the throne [all-under-the-heaven]," Mencius denies the idea that Yao gave the throne to Shun. He explains Shun's succession as a result of Heaven's will (i.e., "Heaven gave it to him"), thereby seeking the ultimate authority in the Mandate of Heaven (*WM*, 354). Thus, we would regard the outcome of *Datong* democracy as the way in which Heaven reveals its own will.

Here, it seems necessary to note the vivid description of *Datong* democracy in *WM*, first, the succession from Yao to Shun:

> After the death of Yâo [Yao], when the three years' mourning was completed, Shun withdrew from the son of Yâo to the south of South river. The princes of the kingdom, however, repairing to court, went not to the son of Yâo, but they went to Shun. Litigants went not to the son of Yâo, but they went to Shun. Singers sang not the son of Yâo, but they sang Shun. (*WM*, 357)

The same kind of passage appears repeatedly when Yu succeeded Shun and Qi (啓), the son of Yu, succeeded Yu:

Shun died. When the three years' mourning was expired, Yü [Yu] withdrew from the son of Shun to Yangch'ăng. The people of the kingdom followed him just as after the death of Yâo [Yao], instead of following his son, they had followed Shun. Yü presented Yî [Yi 益] to Heaven. Seven years elapsed, and Yü died. When the three years' mourning was expired, Yî withdrew from the son of Yü to the north of Mount Ch'î [Qi 啓]. The princes, repairing to court, went not to Yî, but they went to Ch'î. Litigants did not go to Yî, but they went to Ch'î, saying, "He is the son of our sovereign." The singers did not sing Yî, but they sang Ch'î, saying, "He is the son of our sovereign." (*WM*, 358-59)

As I have shown, one of the most crucial political decisions–that is, the election of Shun, Yu, and Qi as the next sovereign–was made by following the principle of *Datong* spelled out in the Great Plan. Of course, this decision has a strong democratic implication, as it includes the people's participation as a necessary component. Whereas the elections of Shun and Yu were the result of overlapping great consensus among the three major parties, the election of Qi was not, but was rather the consensus of princes and officers and the people overruling the presentation of Yi by the preceding sovereign Yu.

It is baffling to note that there has not been an elaborate analysis of Qi's election among Confucian scholars, especially with regard to the question of whether his election should be regarded as hereditary or not in a stricter sense. Nevertheless, it merits our serious attention in two respects. First, although Yi was initially presented to Heaven as the next sovereign by the choice of Yu, Yu's son Qi was elected as the next sovereign by the consensus of the nobles and the people after Yu's death. This bewildering outcome–in which the process was one of democratic competition for the support of nobles and the people, but the result was one of hereditary succession–raises a thorny question as to whether Qi's succession should be considered that of inheritance or that of the transfer to the worthiest, for Qi competed with Yi over the support of nobles and people to ascend to the throne. Second, this episode incidentally pronounces the strong democratic potential and implication that the wills of nobles and the people are more decisive than the will of the sovereign in the process of reaching overlapping consensus among the three major parties. Mencius accepted the election, taking this as the will of Heaven: "all this was from Heaven, and what could not be brought about by man" (*WM*, 359). After all, the democratic decision to elect Qi ended up virtually becoming a hereditary succession. Mencius still seems to take the outcome as hereditary: "When Heaven gave the kingdom to the worthiest, it was given to the worthiest. When Heaven gave it to the son of the preceding sovereign, it was given to him" (*WM*, 358).

Finally, we cannot ignore that divination signs such as the tortoise and the milfoil were afforded great importance as a way of reading the will of heaven with great impartiality in the passage on *Datong* quoted earlier. However, whereas Mencius gives considerable explanation of the great consensus among the sovereign, nobles and officers, and the people in electing Shun, Yu, and Qi, he is completely silent about the divination signs. With regard to Heaven, he only says, "Heaven does not speak. It simply showed its will by his [Shun's] personal conduct and his [Shun's] conduct of affairs" (*WM*, 355). Then Mencius continues with the illustration of Shun's case:

> He [Yao] caused him [Shun] to preside over the sacrifices, and all the spirits were well pleased with them; thus Heaven accepted him. He caused him to preside over the conduct of affairs, and affairs were well administered, so that the people reposed under him; thus the people accepted him. . . . This sentiment is expressed in the words of the Great Declaration: Heaven sees according as my people see; Heaven hears according as my people hear. (*WM*, 356-57)

Mencius's interpretation of Heaven cited above clearly has a strong democratic implication with contemporary appeal because it is human-centered and rational. This is in line with the secular rationalism of Confucian tradition beginning with Confucius, who seldom mentioned Heaven, divinities, and spirits (*CA*, 191, 201, 217, 240-41).

However, it must be a cursory judgment, of course, that divination signs were ignored as trivial in important decision-making during the reign of Yao, Shun, and Yu in ancient Chinese civilization, about twenty centuries before the time of Mencius. In this regard, we may find evidence of Shun's consultation with divination in the dialogue between Shun and Yu before he asked Yu to ascend to the throne. When he exhorted Yu to take over the throne as regent, he praised Yu's great virtue and admirable achievements and said, "The determinate appointment of Heaven rests on your person; you must eventually ascend the throne of the great sovereign" (*BHD*, 61). Then Yu refused courteously and modestly, saying, "Submit the meritorious ministers one by one to the trial of divination, and let the fortunate indication be followed" (*BHD*, 63). Here Yu's suggestion seems reasonable following the common practice of the time. Yu accepted Shun's exhortation in the end, as Shun revealed that his decision was made on the basis of the principle of *Datong*, including divinations signs:

> Yŭ [Yu], the officer of divination, when the mind has been made up on a subject, then refers it to the great tortoise. Now, in this matter, my mind was determined in the first place. I consulted and deliberated with all my ministers and people, and they were of one accord with me. The spirits signified, their assent, the tortoise and grass having both concurred. Divination, when fortunate, may not be repeated. (*BHD*, 63)[7]

From the dialogue between Shun and Yu cited above we may infer with reasonable assurance that the same process of decision-making by *Datong* including the trial of divination had taken place when Yao and Yu exhorted Shun and Yi, respectively, to ascend the throne, although such concrete phrases were not recorded in the relevant situations in *BHD*. If this interpretation is to be accepted as plausible, then we may reach the conclusion that the transfer of the throne during the reign of Yao, Shun, and Yu fits into the decision-making principle of *Datong* democracy, thereby fulfilling one of the necessary conditions for *Datong* society, "all-under-the-heaven for the

7 This passage is significant in another respect, showing that a preceding sovereign followed the principle of *Datong* democracy even when he recommended the worthiest as regent to Heaven.

public."

Confucius, Mencius, and *Datong* Democracy

Thus far, I have examined how the idea of *Datong* democracy was put into practice in the transfer of the throne during the reign of Yao, Shun, and Yu, relying upon Mencius's account of it. In that process, it was confirmed that the people's support or consent was crucial to the actual working of *Datong* democracy. It is intriguing, however, to note a glaring contrast between Confucius and Mencius toward *Datong* democracy. Whereas Confucius did not mention these episodes revealing *Datong* democracy in his *BHD* (which has a detailed description of the reign of Yao, Shun, and Yu) or in *CA*, Mencius gave a rather elaborate explanation of them in his dialogue with his disciple Wanzhang (萬章) in *WM*. Sima Qian also gave a vivid account of *Datong* democracy with his description of the three cases of succession in *GSR* (10-11, 16, 36). Whereas Confucius introduced the idea of *Datong* in *BHD* (Great Plan) but never suggested any concrete examples in his dialogues and books of his own compilation, Mencius suggested and analyzed the concrete examples of *Datong* democracy but never related his examination directly to the second concept of *Datong* as Great Consensus at all, although he might have had access to *BHD*. This strange contrast, however, shows strongly that Mencius was far more democratic than Confucius, who was more in favor of kingship or aristocracy.

Mencius's support for *Datong* democracy is also revealed in his dialogue with King Xuan (宣) of Qi (齊) when he suggests how to appoint men of talents and virtue and punish criminals only as a matter of necessity and caution:

> When all those about you say, – "This is a man of talents and worth," you may not therefore believe it. When your great officers all say, – "This is a man of talents and virtue," neither may you for that [*sic*] believe it. When all the people say, – "This is a man of talents and virtue," then examine into [*sic*] the case, and when you find that the man is such, employ him. When all those about you say, – "This man won't do," don't listen to them. When all your great officers say, – "This man won't do," don't listen to them. When the people all say, – "This man won't do," then examine into [*sic*] the case, and when you find that the man won't do, send him away. When all those about you say, – "This man deserves death," don't listen to them. When all your great officers say, – "This man deserves death," don't listen to them. When the people all say, – "This man deserves death," then inquire into the case, and when you see that the man deserves death, put him to death. In accordance with this we have the saying, "The people killed him." (*WM*, 165-66)

In this passage, we find that Mencius recommends that in employing and dismissing officers and punishing criminals, the king follow the principle of *Datong* democracy; that is, a cumulative consensus-building process leading to a great concord among ministers, the people, and the king. But we cannot find such a passage in *CA*.

Finally, how should we interpret the strong contrast? Concrete examples expressing *Datong* democracy are not present in *BHD* or

CA, whereas Mencius describes it in detail in his *WM*.[8] Besides, we cannot ascertain why and on what authority Mencius included such episodes and his own interpretation in his work. We may only presume that such episodes or myths had been widely circulated over a long time and that Mencius included them and his own interpretation of them because he thought them proper and necessary in his work, whereas Confucius excluded them from his works as unnecessary and improper and never mentioned them in *CA*. Granting that both thinkers were well aware of them, we may therefore interpret that Confucius deliberately chose an elitist "oblivion," whereas Mencius restored and maintained a radical, democratic "recollection."

Confucius's antipopulist (antidemocratic) attitude in contrast to Mencius's is also confirmed in his significant omission of an important historical episode. King Li (厲; c. 864-828 BCE) of Zhou (周) acted cruelly and extravagantly. He was also arrogant and covetous, and he monopolized profits. Thus, when the people in the capital criticized the king's misdeeds, he became furious. So he hired a shaman who watched for criticism. Whomever he reported was put to death and then the criticism was stifled. Given that his ruthless policy continued for a long time, "No one in the capital dared to say a word, but only glanced at each other on the roads" (*GSR*, 71). So the king was delighted in the successful suppression of the people's complaints, saying to the Duke of Zhao (召), "I was able to stop the criticism. Now they dare not speak" (*GSR*, 71). The Duke advanced a remonstrance with strong democratic implication to the king, which

8 However, such episodes are not recorded in other texts of ancient Confucianism including *Xunzi* (荀子) or other books of historiography.

two books of historiography, *GSR* (*Shi Ji* 史記) and *Guo Yu* (國語), describe at length in a vivid voice. For instance, the remonstrance in *GSR* is worth quoting at length:

> This is [merely] blocking up the criticism. To block people's mouths is worse than blocking a river. When an obstructed river bursts its banks, it will surely hurt a great number of people. People are like this, too. For this reason, those who regulate rivers dredge them and let them flow; those who regulate people broaden [channels] and let them talk. Thus when a Son of Heaven presides over the government, from dukes and ministers [down] to [high-] ranking patricians, he makes them offer poems, [he makes] the Blind Musician offer songs, the Scribe offer records, lesser tutors offer admonitions, the blind offer rhapsodies or recitations, the hundred officers offer remonstrations, the common people pass their messages [to the king], close subjects present their corrections, and relatives amend or look into [the king's mistakes]. After the Blind Musician and the Scribe have given their instructions and the elders have ratified them, then the king deliberates on them. Because of this, things can be put into practice without opposition. People having mouths is similar to the land having mountains and rivers, from which the daily needs are drawn. . . . As people have thoughts in their minds and express them through their mouths, if [the ideas] are constructive, you should finish them and put them into practice. If you gag their mouths, how many of them would support [you]? (GSR, 71-72)[9]

9 A similar remonstrance the Duke of Zhao (召) advanced to King Li (厲) appears in a dialogue between the marquis of Tsin [Jin 晉] and the music master Kwang [曠] in *The Ch'un Ts'ew with The Tso Chuen* (春秋左氏傳).

But the king would not listen to his remonstration. Then, three years later, people joined together in revolt and attacked the king, who then fled to Zhi (彘) where he later died (*GSR*, 72). This event corresponds to a passage suggesting the legitimacy of the overthrow of kings and other rulers in the description of Little Prosperity (*Xiaokang* 小康): "Those who do not follow *Li* (禮: rituals), even of high positions, will be removed, as they should be considered a public disaster." In other words, it was a people's revolution overthrowing a despotic king. Here, the remonstration of the Duke of Zhao and the popular revolution have great democratic significance. In particular, the Duke's remonstration merits our attention in the sense that he advocated the maximization of the people's democratic participation according to the principle "everyone according to his due and status";

When the marquis of Tsin [Jin 晉] said to the music master Kwang, "Have not the people of Wei [衛] done very wrong in expelling their rulers?" Kwang defended such an event by replying, "Perhaps the ruler had done very wrong. . . . of what use is he [a bad ruler], and what should they [the people] do but send him away?" Then he suggests how people of every description should conduct themselves in order to correct the defects of their government and watch over the character of their government:

> The historiographers make their records; the blind make their poems; the musicians recite their satires and remonstrances; the great officers admonish and instruct, and inferior officers report to these what they hear; the common people utter their complaints; the merchants [display their wares] in the market places; the hundred artificers exhibit their skilful contrivances. Hence in one of the Books of Hea (Shoo III, iv, iii) it is said, "The herald with this wooden-tongued bell goes along the roads, proclaiming, 'Ye officers, able to instruct, be prepared with your admonitions. Ye workmen engaged in mechanical affairs, remonstrate on the subject of your business.' In the first month at the beginning of spring, that was done. It was done, lest remonstrances should not be regularly presented. Heaven's love for the people is very great; would it allow the one man to take his will and way over them, so indulging his excessive desires and discarding the [kindly] nature of Heaven and Earth? Such a thing could not be." (Book IX Year XIV Duke Seang; Confucius 1960c, 466-67)

that is, *Datong* democracy.

In contrast, Confucius neglected or omitted the remonstrance of the Duke of Zhao and the overthrow of King Li (厲) by the popular revolt. If he had been in favor of *Datong* democracy at all, he could have incorporated this episode when he compiled *BHD*. However, because he was skeptical of or opposed to the political capacity of the people, he presumably sought oblivion by omission, fearing that their introduction would encourage and incite popular revolt.

This attitude of Confucius is further confirmed in the passage where he mentioned different aspects of politics varying with the observance of right principles:

> When right principles (*dao*: 道) prevail in the empire, ceremonies, music, and punitive military expeditions proceed from the son of Heaven. When right principles do not prevail in the empire, ceremonies, music and punitive military expeditions proceed from the princes. . . . When right principles prevail in the kingdom, government will not be in the hands of the great officers. When right principles prevail in the kingdom, there will be no discussions among the common people. (*CA*, 310)

Here, the sentence "When right principles prevail in the kingdom, there will be no discussions among the common people" merits our attention, for it suggests Confucius's low opinion of the political competence of the common people to discuss political affairs.[10] Zhuxi (朱熹) attaches a note to this passage, stating,

10 However, according to the description of *The Confucian Analects*, it should

"This does not mean to muzzle the people to suppress their speech, as Confucius only means by this that there would be no private discussion of politics if there were not bad governance." This interpretation would be plausible, except that we find the common assumption shared by Confucius and Zhuxi to be antidemocratic in the sense that the discussion of political affairs by the common people implies the absence of right principles in the kingdom (i.e., that the kingdom is not ruled properly) or, conversely, that the fact that the common people do not discuss politics signifies the kingdom is ruled properly. In contrast, we are reminded that the Duke of Zhao stressed that the free discussion of politics by people of every description–including the king's relatives and officers–is a necessary condition for good governance, when he remonstrated the king to open various channels allowing the people to raise their voices. That is, the "good governance as outcome" would be secured only by "good governance as procedure."

However, Confucius and Zhuxi took the political quiescence of the people as a desirable state of affairs resulting from good governance. Of course, the two thinkers might have classified the political silence of the masses into two categories: one as a consequence of the popular contentment with good government and the other as that of political suppression by misgovernment. They then might have asserted that what they mean by political silence refers to the former.[11] When we consider the mainstream Confucian

be noted, Confucius was open-minded in giving education to the common people.

11 This has something to do with the contemporary debate in liberal democracy as to whether the political apathy or quiescence of the mass public should be

tradition that regards people as the object of politics, not as their subject, Confucius and Zhuxi are not exceptional on this point. However, it is important to remember there were statesmen like the Duke of Zhao who understood and stressed that popular discussion of and participation in politics was a necessary condition for good government. However, Confucius seems to have taken the option to omit this memory from the Confucian tradition, which would be established fully after his death.

A Radical Remembrance of *Datong* Democracy by Jeong Yakyong after a Long Oblivion

A radical remembrance of *Datong* democracy in the Confucian tradition was not completely disrupted by the silence of Confucius and other mainstream Confucian thinkers, but it has continued to emerge occasionally in words by such figures as the Duke of Zhao (召) and Mencius. In this sense, "On the Origin of Ministers" (原牧) and "Discussing Tang" (湯論), the two fragments written by Jeong Yakyong, could also be cited as a radical recollection of a lost tradition of *Datong* democracy after a long oblivion since Mencius.

First of all, Jeong raises a radical question in the beginning of "On the Origin of Ministers": "Does the minister exist for the people or the people for the minister?" Then he declares that "the minister exists for the people," arguing that the rightful power is created by the

seen as tacit consent coming from contentment or tacit dissent arising from a deep sense of political alienation.

consensus and installation of the people in accordance with *Datong* democracy. Thus, he describes how power is formed from the bottom up through this principle. In the beginning the people set up an impartial person with learning and virtue as their leader who then settles the disputes among them. As the geographical unit expands, the head is set up and installed sequentially from the bottom up: village head → county magistrate → provincial chief → city prince → regional lord → majestic emperor. Stressing that the origin of the emperor lies in the village head and reconfirming that the minister exists for the people, he asserts the application of *Datong* democracy in making laws as well as setting up the political leader:

> The village head formulates a law according to the wishes of the people and submits it to the county magistrate, who then sets up a law according to the wishes of the people and submits it to the provincial chief, who then submits it to the city prince, who then submits it to the majestic emperor. Thus, all the laws made in such a way were very convenient and suitable for the people. (*Collected Works of Jeong Yakyong:* 與猶堂全書)

However, in the later period a man sets up himself as the emperor. Then, from the top down, he appoints his family, relatives, and close cliques as feudal lords, then those lords set up their close attendants as provincial chiefs, and this process repeats itself in appointing county magistrates and village heads. As a consequence, Jeong lamented that rulers make the laws according to their selfish motives and exploit people, so that now "people appear to exist for the minister." As a Confucian scholar, he never relinquished his Confucian belief that the virtuous should rule, and he continued to stress that the rule of the virtuous should be accompanied by the process and principle of *Datong* democracy in which rulers should be verified and set up democratically from the bottom up by the support and consent of the people.

Jeong's idea of *Datong* democracy is articulated again in his fragment "Discussing Tang," in which he discusses whether it is right for Tang (of Yin 殷) to attack and expel King Jie (桀; of Xia 夏); that is, whether it is right for a subject to strike and overthrow a king. In order to examine this, he first notes that the case of a subject's overthrow of a king is not confined to Tang's case only but can be traced back to the legendary origin of Chinese history, in which Huang-di (黃帝: The Yellow Emperor) ascended to the throne as the Son of Heaven. According to Sima Qian's description in the "Basic Annals of the Five Emperors" in *GSR* (Shi Ji 史記), Xuan-yuan (軒轅), a mere subject, defeated Yan-di (炎帝: The Flaming Emperor) in a series of battles and finally ascended to the throne as the Huang-di. Thus he argues that the fact that a subject attacked and expelled a king is not as important as the issue of whether the subject was enthroned to the Son of Heaven with or without the support of the people and feudal lords. In order to support this point, he advances a similar theory as to the status and origin of the Son of Heaven that is developed in the fragment "On the Origin of Ministers." According to his explanation, political leaders are set up by the people's support from the bottom up: neighborhood chief → village head → county magistrate ⊠ regional lord ⊠ Son of Heaven.

Furthermore, Jeong argues that it is natural that political

leaders of each level elected from the bottom up be replaced by the deliberation of members of the lower political unit who elected them before. Thus, he maintains that the principle remains the same, whether five families replace a neighborhood chief through mutual consultation or nine overlords and eight lords replace a Son of Heaven by mutual consultation. Thus, following this logic, he retorts, "Who could say that a subject attacks and expels a king?" In this way, Jeong asserts that it is legitimate that people of a lower political unit who elected their political leaders can expel them by their own consultation and agreement.

In addition, Jeong reverses the common understanding of "observant of the order" (*shun* 順: obedient) and "against the order" (*ni* 逆: rebellious) in his time on the basis of his argument developed in the two fragments:

> The Son of Heaven has appointed feudal lords; the lord, the county magistrates; the county magistrate, village heads; and the village head, the neighborhood chiefs since the Han empire. So if people dare not to be respectful of their superior, then they are called "against the order." However, what do we mean by "against the order"? In olden ages, as the people below set up the people above, it was "observant of the order." Now, as the people above appoint the people below, it is "against the order." Thus Wang Mang (王莽), Cao Cao (曹操), Sima Yi (司馬懿), Liu Yu (劉裕), Xiao Yan (蕭衍), and so on are "against the order," and King Wu (武王), King Tang (湯王), and Emperor Huang-di (黃帝) were wise kings and sage emperors. (*Collected Works of Jeong Yakyong:* 與猶堂全書)

According to Jeong's principle of *Datong* democracy, as explicitly stated in this quotation, the prevalent convention by which those above appointed those below is now "against the order," whereas the old practice by which those below set up those above is "observant of the order." Thus, he has subverted the then-prevailing understanding of "observant of the order" and "against the order" and sought to restore the principle of *Datong* democracy in a radical way by resurrecting its memory glimmering in ancient Confucianism.

In addition to Jeong, when some Japanese and Chinese Confucian intellectuals agonized over radical reform or revolution to transform traditional Confucian monarchy and introduce a republican or democratic form of government in the late nineteenth century, they welcomed and hailed American democracy with its presidential system as an alternative form of governance, equating it with the legendary Yao-Shun reign in ancient China. Shimada Genji (島田虔次) notes in his article "Yao-Shun Democracy?" [堯舜民主政?] that Yokoi Shonan (横井小楠, 1809-69), a Japanese intellectual, sought republicanism under the influence of Yao-Shun and glorified American presidential government. Finding that the position of president as the head of the state was not inherited but chosen by mass election, he severely criticized succession by blood and praised succession by election, which reminded him of Yao-Shun's voluntary abdication and transfer of the throne (Shimada 1997, 78-80).

Likewise, Chinese intellectuals and activists who dreamed of radical reform or revolution in the late nineteenth century and praised democracy compared Yao and Shun with American presidents. This is confirmed by the statement of Liang Qi-chao (梁啓超, 1873-1929): "Those who mention modern people's rights and *Datong* have praised Yao and Shun, thereby seeking to demonstrate the existence of democracy in ancient China" (quoted in Shimada 1997, 89).

Citing and interpreting scattered phrases related to *minben* (民本: "of the people" or people-centered) and democracy in Confucian classics such as *The Book of Historical Documents*, *The Ch'un Ts'ew with The Tso Chuen*, *The Works of Mencius*, *The Rites of Zhou* (周禮), and the like, Liang Qi-chao himself drew democratic implications from *Datong* in the Great Plan, as I have done in this chapter:

> Through these examples and episodes, we may suppose the existence of assemblies by all citizens as they were in ancient Greek poleis. As the size of population was small, this was actually possible. The phrase "consult with the masses of the people" [謀及庶人] in the Great Plan approaches this method. . . . The ancient people held the right to participate at least in decision-making for the three important political affairs–the threat to the security of the state, setting-up of a king, and the transfer of capital. It was, however, naturally impossible to put this method into practice in a large populous country. Thus, we have not been able to discuss its plausibility in the political situation since the time of the Warring States period. To summarize, our ancestors recognized well that the people's will should be respected, but did not continuously ponder over the question of how to realize the people's will in actual practice. (Liang Qi-chao 2012, 34-37)

Here it is important to note that Liang did not conclude that the experience of democracy was completely absent from Chinese history, but that it was present in part. In other words, his conclusion was that whereas the tradition of *minben* existed consistently and continuously in Chinese history, the tradition of democracy was inchoate, disrupted, but never recovered. Thus, Confucian idealism or radicalism sparked by the Western impact in the late nineteenth century found the idea of *Datong* democracy once again along the image of Yao-Shun's reign through radical recollection among East Asian intellectuals.

Concluding Remarks

Thus far, I have articulated the idea of *Datong* democracy dispersed in various Confucian texts and the historiography of ancient China and Jeong Yakyong's two fragments. The idea was, however, recollected radically by some East Asian Confucian intellectuals in the late nineteenth century who were groping for a democratic or republican political system as an alternative to Confucian monarchy in the face of Western civilization. But their appeal to the idea of *Datong* democracy remained somewhat vague, simply equating Yao-Shun's voluntary abdication of the throne as democracy without further elaboration. This chapter has imparted, however, more theoretical substance to *Datong* democracy by conducting a more elaborate analysis of Confucian texts and explaining the two ideas of *Datong* together, their close relation having been rather ignored before. Nevertheless, it has some serious problems as a preliminary overview, which I want to spell out to suggest some guidelines for future research.

First of all, the question may be raised as to whether *Datong* democracy suggested in this chapter is properly conceptualized and can thus be defined as *democracy*. Recognizing this difficulty, I extended the concept of democracy to incorporate a republican form of government in which a king, nobles, and citizens share political power. Further theoretical endeavor seems necessary, however, to impart an institutional form to it, a task that also requires the contribution of historical and archaeological research.

Second, if we examine the actual history of republics and democracies of the ancient Orient and Greece, we find that those polities presupposed the existence of vigorous and numerous citizens who were engaged in commerce and other trades and free to participate in politics as well as the prosperity of urban civilization, which led to a vibrant society. Thus, we need to find the historical evidence that urban civilization with politically active citizenship existed and prospered in ancient China in order to prove that democratic forms of government existed there.

Finally, this chapter has only been successful in articulating the "idea" of *Datong* democracy through the textual analysis of Chinese Confucian and historical texts. Thus, to make the argument that a certain form of democracy actually existed in ancient Chinese civilization, we need to prove that some democratic institutions such as a bicameral deliberative assembly (senate and popular assembly), "rule of law," "procedures for holding magistrates to account and trial by jury," the "rotation of magistracies," and "voting by ballot and by lot" were found widely in China as well (Springborg 1992, 3). In order to overcome these limitations, we need to be assisted by the positive achievement of recent research in the fields of archaeology and epigraphy, including the study of inscriptions on bones and tortoise carapaces, as well as history.

References

English Materials

Bernal, Martin. 1987. *Black Athena: The Afroasiatic Roots of Classical Civilization*. Vol. 1. New Brunswick, NJ: Rutgers University Press.

Confucius. 1960a. *The Confucian Analects, the Great Learning, the Doctrine of the Mean*. Vol. 1 of *The Chinese Classics*, edited and translated by James Legge, 137-354. Hong Kong: Hong Kong University Press.

——. 1960b. *The Shoo King or The Book of Historical Documents*. Vol. 3 of *The Chinese Classics*, edited and translated by James Legge. Hong Kong: Hong Kong University Press.

——. 1960c. *The Ch'un Ts'ew with The Tso Chuen*. Vol. 5 of *The Chinese Classics*, edited and translated by James Legge. Hong Kong: Hong Kong University Press.

Finley, Moses I. 1973. *Democracy Ancient and Modern*. New Brunswick, NJ: Rutgers University Press.

——. 1983. *Politics in the Ancient World*. Cambridge: Cambridge University Press.

Mencius. 1960. *The Works of Mencius*. Vol. 2 of *The Chinese Classics*, edited and translated by James Legge. Hong Kong: Hong Kong University Press.

Springborg, Patricia. 1992. *Western Republicanism and the Oriental Prince*. Cambridge, MA: Polity Press.

Ssu-ma Ch'ien [Sima Qian]. 1994. *The Grand Scribe's Records*, edited by William H. Nienhauser, Jr. Vol. 1, *The Basic Annals of Pre-Han*

China, translated by Tsai-fa Cheng, Zongli Lu, William H. Nienhauser, Jr., and Robert Reynolds. Bloomington: Indiana University Press.

Vlassopoulos, Kostas. 2007. *Unthinking the Greek Polis: Ancient Greek History beyond Eurocentrism*. Cambridge: Cambridge University Press.

Wolff, Eric. 1982. *Europe and the People without History*. Berkeley: University of California Press.

Chinese / Korean Classical Texts

國語. *Guo Yu*

與猶堂全書. *Yeoyudangjeonseo* [*Collected Works of Jeong Yakyong*]

禮記集說大全. *The Book of Rituals*

Chinese and Japanese Materials

Liang, Qi-chao [梁啓超]. 2012.『先秦政治思想史』[The History of Pre-Qin Political Thought]. Beijing: Zhongguo Renmin University Press.

Shimada, Genji (島田虔次). 1997. "堯舜民主政？" [Yao-Shun Democracy?]『隠者の尊重: 中国の歴史哲学』[Respect for Hidden People: Philosophy of History in China]. Tokyo: Chikumashobo.

Korean Materials

Huang, Zongxi. 2000. *Myeongidaebangnok* [Expectation of a New Age]. Translated by Deok-gyun Kim. Seoul: Hangilsa.

Chapter 6

Reexamining Rousseau's Political Thought: Does Citizens' Political Participation Include Public Discussions and Debates?

Jean-Jacques Rousseau is known among modern Western political theorists as the strongest advocate of popular sovereignty and the most consistent defender of direct democracy through active civic participation.[1] However, the baffling paradox remains that most Western commentators—contrary to wide popular assumption—interpret Rousseau as denying citizens the ability to participate in politics through forms of public interaction such as discussion and debate. Rousseau's work—notably his celebrated *Social Contract*—contains certain passages that seem to deny citizens the right to active public interaction, so it remains unclear whether citizens are allowed to engage in such interaction in the process of finding the general will

1 Of course, Rousseau accepts and prescribes representative democracy on a national level to make allowances for the size of the territory and the population in a given state in *Considerations on the Government of Poland.*

and making it into law. One of the most typical and frequently cited passages regarding this question is found in book II, chapter 3, of *The Social Contract*: "If, when an adequately informed people deliberates, the citizens were to have no communication among themselves, the general will would always result from the large number of small differences, and the deliberation would always be good" (II, iii, 61).[2]

If citizens were denied public interaction and political participation in civic assemblies, and therefore were confined to voting for or against given legislative propositions, Rousseau's strong advocacy of direct democracy would lose a great deal of its purport and significance. Careful examination of *The Social Contract*, *Considerations on the Government of Poland* (hereafter, *Considerations*), and Rousseau's other political writings, however, reveals that discussion and debate are allowed under certain conditions; that is, according to "type of the state" and subject to certain regulations.[3] I therefore oppose the conventional negative interpretation according to which Rousseau comprehensively forbids discussion and debate, taking instead the position that it is crucial, in evaluating Rousseau's direct democracy, to note the public civic discussion that his political thought allows.

2 This passage will be analyzed in more detail later in the chapter. Hereafter, I refer to this passage as "P1," because it is cited frequently. The text used for *The Social Contract* in this chapter is Jean-Jacques Rousseau, *On the Social Contract with Geneva Manuscript and Political Economy*, ed. Roger D. Masters and Judith R. Masters (New York: St. Martin's Press, 1978). Whenever *The Social Contract* is cited here, the parenthetical reference will give book, chapter, and page.

3 The meaning of the phrase "subject to certain regulations" will be elaborated later in the chapter.

In order to develop and defend my positive interpretation, I first classify the types of state described in *The Social Contract* in terms of degree of corruption and variety of civic participation. I then offer various interpretations with regard to the question of whether Rousseau's citizens are allowed to engage in active public interaction in assemblies, before placing these interpretations into negative and positive categories. Finally, I seek to refute negative interpretations and support the positive one on the basis of my reading of Rousseau's major works.

Rousseau's Classification of Types of State: Degree of Corruption and Variety of Political Participation

In book IV, chapter 1, of *The Social Contract*, Rousseau classifies types of state primarily in terms of degree of corruption. Aspects and consequences of civic political participation appear to vary according to the type of state. After presenting his typology of the state, Rousseau offers his main point: "It can be seen from the preceding chapter that the way in which general matters are handled can provide a rather precise indication of the current state of the mores and health of the body politic" (IV, ii, 109). The major assumption of this chapter is thus that we must examine whether civic participation includes public discussion and debate, according to the type of state. I identify four types of state in *The Social Contract* by considering passages in book II, chapter 3, and book IV, chapter 2, although Rousseau presents only three types in book IV, chapter 1.

The validity of this addition will be confirmed through the subsequent development of my interpretation.

The Ideal State: A Healthy Peasant Community (Type 1)

Rousseau describes as the happy and ideal state the simple and honest community in which a group of peasants as "a single body" manages its common affairs according to "a single will which relates to their common preservation and the general welfare." In such a community, "the common good is clearly apparent everywhere, and requires only good sense to be perceived" (IV, i, 108). Here, as citizens do not pursue their private interests or form small factions or associations, there are no clashes between the general will and the particular wills of individual citizens, so that unanimous decisions can be reached without trouble. Given that the citizens are uncorrupted and the common good is easy to discern, they decide upon the affairs of state wisely. Rousseau describes how they are dealt with as follows:

> A State governed in this way needs very few laws, and to the degree that it becomes necessary to promulgate new ones, this necessity is universally seen. The first to propose them merely states what everyone has already felt, and there is no question of intrigues nor of eloquence to pass into law what each has already resolved to do as soon as he is sure that others will do likewise. (IV, i, 108)

The Semi-Ideal State: The Early Roman Republic (Type 2)

Rousseau regards the early Roman republic as a kind of semi-ideal state, not able to reach the level of the ideal state described in the previous section. While recognizing the confrontation of the patricians and plebeians "whose quarrels often disturbed the comitia even in the finest period" of the Roman republic and diagnosing this as deriving from problems inherent in the constitution itself, he still stresses that "even in the stormiest times, the plebiscites of the people, when the senate did not interfere with them, always passed calmly and by a large majority of votes. Since the citizens had only one interest, the people had only one will" (IV, ii, 109-10). Thus, according to Rousseau, although some Roman plebeians pursued individual private interests, excluding the possibility of unanimous will, they were still able to pass resolutions by a large majority because they were not yet divided into factions or parties.

Rousseau's description of the early Roman republic shows that he recognized it as being, overall, a healthy body politic, albeit one that fell short of the ideal peasant state. Rousseau appears to think that, insofar as small parties and associations around which private interests partially cohere have not formed, the general will would prevail at least by a large majority, if not with unanimity. Such is the difference between the ideal and the semi-ideal state. Rousseau thus states: "In order for the general will to be well expressed, it is therefore important that there be no partial society in the State, and that each citizen give only his own opinion" (II, iii, 61). He describes the deliberation process as follows:

> If, when an adequately informed people deliberates, the citizens were to have no communication among themselves, the general will would always result from the large number of small differences, and the deliberation would always be good. (II, iii, 61)[4]

Here, Rousseau elaborates on the meaning of the "large number of small differences" deriving from each citizen's own opinion or private will:

> There is often a great difference between the will of all and the general will. The latter considers only the common interest: the former considers private interest, and is only a sum of private wills. But take away from these same wills the pluses and minuses that cancel each other, and the remaining sum of the differences is the general will. (II, iii, 61)

This passage reinforces my point that the category of semi-ideal state is independent and distinct from that of the ideal state, by showing additionally that the way the general will is found in the former is different from that in the latter.

4 "Si, quand le peuple suffisamment informé délibére, les Citoyens n'avoient aucune communication entre eux, du grand nombre de petites différences résulteroit toujours la volonté générale, et la délibération seroit toujours bonne" (Rousseau 1964, *Du Contrat Social*, II, iii, 371).

The Considerably Corrupt State (Type 3)

In Rousseau's political theory, any state that is healthy to begin with is inevitably susceptible to corruption and decline. He thus depicts civic participation in a state with considerable corruption:

> But when the social tie begins to slacken and the State to grow weak; when private interests start to make themselves felt and small societies to influence the large one, the common interest changes and is faced with opponents; unanimity no longer prevails in the votes; the general will is no longer the will of all; contradictions and debates arise and the best advice is not accepted without disputes. (IV, i, 108)

Here, the decisive difference between the semi-ideal state and the considerably corrupt state seems to be whether small parties, associations, and societies are formed in the body politic. In the latter state, citizens now start to form small societies and participate in politics, pursuing private interests (or particular wills) of individuals and small societies rather than the general will. Rousseau thus distinguishes such a state from ideal and semi-ideal states:

> One can say, then, that there are no longer as many voters as there are men, but merely as many as there are associations. The differences become less numerous and produce a result that is less general. (II, iii, 61)

Rousseau makes a similar contrast elsewhere:

> The more harmony there is in the assemblies, that is, the closer opinions come to obtaining unanimous support, the more dominant as well is the general will. But long debates, dissensions, and tumult indicate the ascendance of private interests and the decline of the State. (IV, ii, 109)

In a state where corruption has advanced to a considerable degree, the will of all cannot undergo the mutual cancellation of individual wills necessary to obtain the general will, making the latter a rarity. As the passage "the best advice is not accepted without disputes" suggests, however, this does not mean that the general will is disregarded completely. Rousseau's solution for letting the general will prevail in such a body politic is to restore it artificially to a condition closer to that of the semi-ideal state, suggesting that "if there are partial societies, their number must be multiplied and their inequality prevented" (II, iii, 61). If such a measure were successful, the will of all would approximate to the general will through the mutual cancellation effect, with resolutions passed by a large majority.

The Severely Corrupt State (Type 4)

Finally, Rousseau describes political participation and its consequences in a severely corrupt state:

> Finally, when the State, close to its ruin, continues to subsist only in an illusory and ineffectual form; when the social bond is broken in all hearts; when the basest interest brazenly adopts the

> sacred name of the public good, then the general will becomes mute; all–guided by secret motives–are no more citizens in offering their opinions than if the State had never existed, and iniquitous decrees whose only goal is the private interest are falsely passed under the name of laws. (IV, i, 109)

In such a severely corrupt state, as a consequence of the failure of Rousseau's solution, the number of small societies decreases and the equality among them breaks down completely: "Finally when one of these associations is so big that it prevails over all the others, the result is no longer a sum of small differences, but a single difference. Then there is no longer a general will, and the opinion that prevails is merely a private opinion" (II, iii, 61).

In book IV, chapter 2, of *The Social Contract,* Rousseau describes the mode of political participation and its consequence when corruption reaches its extreme point, citing the case of the abject state of the Roman senate under the emperors:

> At the other extreme, unanimity returns. That is when the citizens, fallen into servitude, no longer have either freedom or will. Then fear and flattery turn voting into acclamations. Men no longer deliberate; they adore or they curse. (IV, ii, 110)

Because a few factions (or just a single faction) occupy the dominant position in the state, the remaining, powerless citizens are overwhelmed by this dominant faction(s) and unable to frankly express opposite or different opinions. They merely engage in "curse[s]" or "flattery," out of sheer fear.[5]

Among these four types, the ideal and semi-ideal states are those in which simplicity and honesty would prevail among mostly healthy citizens. The early Roman republic and Sparta before its decline, in which small societies had not formed, seem to correspond to the semi-ideal state. Political decisions are made unanimously in the ideal state but by majority vote in the semi-ideal state, for there is some embryonic corruption among the citizens in the latter. In considerably and severely corrupt states, in contrast, most citizens have lost their simplicity and honesty. Athens, the later Roman republic, and Rome in its imperial stage would correspond to these. Partial societies and factions form in both types: In the considerably corrupt state, their number is still plural, they balance one another, and their influence is dispersed; whereas, in the severely corrupt state their number is reduced to a few or one, and their influence is severely skewed in favor of the few or monopolized by a single faction. If we compare the four types of state in terms of expression of the general will in relation to the will of all, there are interesting differences to be noted. Whereas the will of all is naturally identical to the general will in the ideal state, and the former turns artificially (i.e., by mutual cancellation of individual wills) into the latter in the semi-ideal state, the general will is rarely expressed in the considerably corrupt state and, when it is, this is often not inevitable but accidental. Obviously, the will of all or the majority does not coincide with the general will at all in a severely corrupt state.

5 Therefore, Rousseau prescribes that the decision-making procedure should change from public to secret voting as the healthy body politic turns into a corrupt state (IV, iv, 119).

Does Civic Political Participation Include Public Discussion and Debate? Overview of Existing Interpretations

Now we may turn to the main subject of this chapter. Although the question of whether civic political participation includes public discussion and debate is more complicated than is usually assumed, not many commentators explicitly examine this question and come up with their own interpretation. In addition, most commentators who manage to advance explicit interpretations take the negative position that Rousseau does not allow public discussion and debate. In contrast, my ultimate interpretation in this chapter is the positive one that Rousseau's citizens are allowed to engage in active public interaction according to type of state and subject to certain regulations. Without allowing public interaction, I assert, the true value of Rousseau's direct democracy would not be realized or appreciated at all. In order to argue the validity of my position, a persuasive refutation of the aforementioned negative position is needed. I thus summarize the critical passages at issue in *The Social Contract,* before surveying negative and positive interpretations in this section. Finally, in the next section, I advance my critique of negative positions and elaborate my positive alternative.

Crucial passages cited to support negative interpretations are P1 in book II, chapter 3; the passage in which civic public interaction is described as almost unnecessary in the ideal state portrayed in book IV, chapter 1; and the passage in which "long debates, dissensions, and tumult" are described negatively as indicating "the ascendance of private interests and the decline of the State" in book IV, chapter 2. In addition, there is a critical but ambiguous passage that seems to validate the negative interpretation but, in my opinion, actually suggests the probability that active civic public deliberation is allowed. This passage merits quotation at length:

> I could make many comments here about the simple right to vote in every act of sovereignty–a right that nothing can take away from the citizens; and on the right to give an opinion, to make propositions, to analyze, to discuss, which the government is always very careful to allow only to its members. But this important subject would require a separate treatise and I cannot say everything in this one. (IV, i, 109; hereafter, "P2")[6]

I will now introduce and examine various interpretations of this subject, before advancing my own. Most of the scholars to be examined take a negative position, except Hilail Gildin and Melissa Schwartzberg, who recently published an article on the subject under the title "Voting the General Will: Rousseau on Decision Rules."

James McAdam, in his article on Rousseau's general will, offers a negative interpretation in consideration of Rousseau's negative view of small associations immediately following P1: "in coming to a decision regarding the General Will, no individual would even communicate his thoughts on the matter to other individuals. His reason for this extraordinary measure is precisely that such exchange of views between individuals encourages the development of partial general

6 Interpretation of this passage will be offered in the next section.

wills which could then be in direct competition with the General Will" (McAdam 1967, 503).[7]

Roger D. Masters, an authoritative commentator on Rousseau's political thought in the United States, also takes a negative position. Masters does not make explicit remarks on P1 in his book *The Political Philosophy of Rousseau* or in his edition of Rousseau's *Social Contract* (Masters 1968, 386ff.; Rousseau 1978). But he quotes P1 elsewhere in order to argue that Rousseau's citizens are not allowed public discussion and debate. In his editorial footnote to P2 in Rousseau's *Social Contract* he states:

> Rousseau's ironical defense of free speech has confused some editors who read the last clause as a serious statement of principle; such an interpretation is unlikely given the next chapter as well as Book II, Chap. 3 [i.e., P1]. (Rousseau 1978, 150n112)

The German social philosopher Habermas, while developing his theory of the public sphere in *The Structural Transformation of the Public Sphere* (1989), gives a negative interpretation that merits our attention for its explicit denial and lengthy elaboration:

> Locke's "Law of Opinion" became sovereign by way of Rousseau's *Contrat Social*. Under the rubric of a different

7 Lester G. Crocker, who edited one of the popular editions of Rousseau's *Social Contract*, offers the same interpretation: "There is no debate or discussion, and each citizen must deliberate in isolation" (Crocker 1967, ix). However, as we shall see later, Bernard Manin denies even the need for isolated deliberation.

> *opinion publique* unpublic opinion was elevated to the status of sole legislator, and this involved the elimination of the public's rational critical debate in the public sphere. The legislative procedure envisaged by Rousseau left no doubt in this regard. *Bon sens* (common sense, *gesunder Menschenverstand*) was all that was needed to perceive the common welfare. The simple people, indeed simpletons, would be merely irritated by the political maneuvers of public discussion: long debates would bring particular interests to the fore. Rousseau contrasted dangerous appeals of silver-tongued orators with the harmony of assemblies. The *volonté générale* was more a consensus of hearts than of arguments. The society was governed best in which the laws (*lois*) corresponded to the already established mores (*opinions*). The simplicity of mores was a protection against "thorny discussions" (*discussions épineuses*), whereas luxury corrupted healthy simplicity, subjugated one group to another and all of them to public opinion (*et tous à l'opinion*). (Habermas 1989, 97-98)

Here, Habermas gives an explicit interpretation, focusing primarily on Rousseau's ideal state, according to which Rousseau's citizens are prohibited from engaging in any communication, including discussion and debate, among themselves. I will not present any additional analysis of Habermas's long quote, for it shows fully his interpretation and the rationale behind his defining of Rousseau's democracy as "democracy of unpublic opinion" or "democracy without public debate" (Habermas 1989, 98-99). As textual evidence to support this interpretation, he refers to book IV, chapters 1 and 2, and book III, chapters 1 and 4, in the footnotes without offering further analysis.

Finally, French political theorist Bernard Manin offers a negative interpretation in his article "On Legitimacy and Political Deliberation" and provides detailed grounds for it. His points can be summarized as follows. First, Manin interprets the word *deliberation* (*délibération, délibérer*) in *The Social Contract* as referring not to the process of citizens communicating with each other and forming a collective will but to the decision itself. As examples to support this, he suggests two passages in book II, chapter 3, and a passage in *Discourse on Political Economy*.[8] One of the two passages in *The Social Contract* is P1, and the other is the following:

> It follows from the preceding that the general will is always right and always tends toward the public good. But it does not follow that the people's deliberations have always the same righteousness [rectitude]. One always wishes for one's own good, but one cannot always see it. The people cannot be corrupted, but they are often deceived, and it is only then that they seem to wish for what is bad. (II, iii, 61)

After quoting this passage, Manin asserts:

> In this passage, the "deliberations of the people" obviously refer to the choices the people make, and not to the process that leads to the choice. There would be no sense in saying that a

8 For the passage in the *Discourse on Political Economy*, see Manin (1987, 345). I shall not elaborate it in this chapter.

process is morally right or not. (Manin 1987, 345)

Second, he suggests that "Rousseau's individuals are already supposed to know what they want when they come to a public assembly to decide in common. They have already determined their will, so that any act of persuasion attempted by others could only taint their will and oppress it" (Manin 1987, 346). In order to support this interpretation, Manin cites the ideal state in book IV, chapter 1, in which "its maxims [are] *clear* and *luminous* . . . the public good would be *evident* everywhere" (emphasis in original). Thus, according to Manin, deliberation that ordinarily presupposes communication of opinions and discussion is a process necessary when the locus of the public good or the general will is uncertain and the collective examination of alternative possibilities is thus required. In Rousseau's ideal state, however, Manin stresses that "what is evident, simple, and luminous does not need to be deliberated in the strong sense of that term" (Manin 1987, 347).[9]

Third, Manin cites Rousseau's argument that criticizes the harmful effect of discussion, debate, and dissension among citizens in state types 3 and 4, where corruption plagues the state to considerable and severe degrees, respectively. Manin interprets Rousseau as rejecting not only discussion and debate but also "the mere communication between citizens," because phenomena such as

9 However, if we take seriously Rousseau's statement quoted herein, "One always wishes for one's own good, but one cannot always see it," may not Rousseau's citizens need some form of deliberation to check whether what they have seen is correct? Opinion is related to the realm of the visible and so is susceptible to deception and self-deception.

the manifestation of special interests, the exercise of undue influence, and flimsy persuasion by eloquent rhetoric provide opportunities for the formation of parties and taint and suppress the will of individual citizens (Manin 1987, 345-47).

In contrast to the negative interpretations so far examined, Gildin and Schwartzberg posit the probability that Rousseauean citizens are (to a certain extent) allowed public discussion and debate; I agree with their position overall. First of all, Gildin interprets the "no communication" clause in P1 as meaning that Rousseau wants to ban "secret agreements" among citizens who are liable to form partial associations and parties, noting their deleterious effect on the expression of the general will. Furthermore, citing a passage from Rousseau's *Letters Written from the Mountain* (hereafter, *Letters*), Gildin advances the interpretation, similar to that of Masters, that Rousseau actually seems to permit citizens public discussion and debate in P2, and, contrary to Masters's perplexity, further argues that this shows Rousseau's flexibility with regard to the citizens' right to submit new laws and debate them:

> His [Rousseau's] remarks have occasioned some perplexity. He clearly declares that the right to vote on laws is an essential part of sovereignty. He has been believed to hold further that the right to bring a new law before the sovereign assembly and to state one's opinion of its merits or disadvantages must be the preserve of government. In the *Letters Written from the Mountain*, however, while he continues to favor reserving to the governing councils of Geneva the right to submit new laws to the sovereign he complains of their denying the sovereign the

right to debate them. (Gildin 1983, 159)

In addition, noting Rousseau's rather unenthusiastic description in P2 of the governmental tendency to reserve the right to submit new laws and to debate them to its members and his strong caution against governmental tyranny and decay encroaching on the freedom of a people, Gildin states conclusively: "Rousseau's remarks [in P2] suggest that there are many possible arrangements regarding the right to propose and to debate laws compatible with his principles" (Gildin 1983, 159).[10]

Although recognizing the significance of P1 and accepting the mainstream interpretation of it, Schwartzberg also carefully advances the interpretation that, while communication among citizens should be banned completely at the time of voting, since this is when it poses the greatest threat, some amount of discussion should be permitted prior to this point (Schwartzberg 2008, 418). On Rousseau's ultimate position over the decision rule, Schwartzberg prefers majoritarian to unanimous rules, saying, "although the votes as a whole ought optimally to approach unanimity, the means by which that might be accomplished is through majoritarian and supermajoritarian rather than unanimous voting rules." This is for moral and other reasons (Schwartzberg 2008, 15). She then argues that majoritarian and supermajoritarian rules require some form of communication among citizens, including discussions, prior to voting. On this interpretation, Schwartzberg maintains that when Rousseau's citizens make voting

10 In order to support this argument, Gildin notes in the previous passage the rights of peasants to propose new laws in the ideal state.

decisions, they ought to carefully reflect on the correctness of their own decision, consider other citizens' opinions from a perspective of humility and their own fallibility, and be willing to revise their own decisions. This task requires the prior knowledge of other citizens' opinions and positions, which is, in turn, to be acquired only by some form of discussion and debate:

> One must be specially concerned to ensure that *amour propre* has not blinded oneself to the general will: in the face of almost universal opposition . . . the prospective voter ought to recognize that one is very likely to be mistaken, and reverse one's vote rather than exercise a veto. However, a representative could not possibly know whether he was actually using his veto power *ex ante*–whether his view was idiosyncratic or in keeping with the other voters–if he did not possess any prior knowledge of others' likely votes. This knowledge, however, could only come from discussion. (Schwartzberg 2008, 417)

Furthermore, noting that correct decisions depend on a people "sufficiently informed" (*suffisamment informé*) according to P1, Schwartzberg still argues that although the "way in which citizens come to know the perspectives of others cannot take the form of rhetorical appeals or vigorous debates, and certainly not bargaining, . . . it must indeed be at least partially a discursive process" (Schwartzberg 2008, 417-18).[11] In short, Schwartzberg's positivist interpretation

11 To reinforce her point, Schwartzberg also calls attention to this passage regarding the ideal state: "There is no need for intrigues or eloquence to secure passage of law of what each has already resolved to do *as soon as he is sure that*

seems quite modest, partly owing to being overwhelmed by Manin's argument, against which she raises her own alternative interpretation.

In order to refute the negative and reinforce the positive interpretation in the next section, it is necessary to summarize the two positions more succinctly. The negativists I have examined, notably Masters, Habermas, and Manin, reach the interpretation that public discussion and debate among citizens are never allowed, regardless of political context and type of state, because they are unnecessary in the ideal state–and even obstructive when it comes to finding expression of the general will in other types of state–by encouraging the formation of small societies around which private interests cohere. First, Masters takes it for granted that P1 supports the negative interpretation without exception, and thus attempts no flexible interpretation of it. When he finds, however, that P2 seems to hint at the right of citizens to submit new laws and debate them, as Gildin's comment suggests, he seems a little embarrassed but still adheres adamantly to his negative position, relying on P1 and pondering P2 no longer.

Habermas advances his negative interpretation on the basis of passages in book III, chapter 4, and book IV, chapters 1 and 2, without directly mentioning P1. When Rousseau discusses democracy in book III, chapter 4, he stipulates as necessary conditions for it (1) a small state, (2) the simplicity of mores that prevents a multitude of

the others will do likewise" (Schwartzberg 2008, 418; IV, i, 108; emphasis in original). She then suggests that, although the common good is so apparent, the confidence ex ante that "others will see the matter similarly" requires a "discursive process." (Schwartzberg 2008, 418) She also raises some more minor points to strengthen her interpretation.

business and thorny discussions, (3) a great equality among citizens, and (4) little or no luxury (III, iv, 85). Thus bearing mostly state types 1 and 4 in mind, Habermas does not hesitate to characterize Rousseau's view of democracy as "democracy without public debate."

Finally, Manin argues strongly that the deliberation of Rousseau's citizens does not include interactive discussion and debate, saying, "the deliberations of the people obviously refer to the choices the people make, and not to the process that leads to the choice." In addition to his own analysis of the meaning of deliberation in *The Social Contract*, Manin suggests that citizens' interactive deliberation is not necessary in state type 1 and that it is even harmful in state type 4.

However, the positivist Gildin takes P2 as Rousseau's principal position and interprets P1 in a rather limited way. But Gildin keeps silent about the way in which Rousseau's citizens engage in lively public interaction and also does not seek to adduce additional textual evidence to support his argument. Schwartzberg also suggests the probability, based on more careful inference and concrete textual evidence, that Rousseau's citizens may need public discussion on occasion, while still respecting the mainstream negative interpretation. But her explication does not go far enough, and thus her interpretation remains confined to pointing to probability–it fails to provide sufficient evidence and the further inference necessary to support it.

Critique of Negative Interpretations and Defense of the Positive Interpretation

According to my examination so far, three issues must be resolved in order to decide whether Rousseau allows public discussion and debate. First, we must relate our subject more closely to the various types of state. Negativists strongly assert their own interpretations and admit no exceptions, relying primarily on Rousseau's negative comments about discussion and debate among citizens and focusing mainly on state types 1 and 4. Positivists, in turn, advance theirs in a very modest and defensive way, not paying close attention to the various types of state.[12] We may well also approve the interpretation, agreed upon by both parties, that interactive communication among citizens such as discussion and debate is unnecessary in state type 1 and even deleterious in state type 4. However, both parties appear to fail to examine with discrimination the question of whether public discussion and debate are permitted in state types 2 and 3, even though we might imagine that public discussion and debate would turn out to be useful and even necessary in these types. Second, it should be decided how consistently we must match the conditional "no communication" clause in P1 with P2, which is rather ambiguous regarding whether Rousseau's citizens are allowed active public interaction. Third, we must search for any important passages in Rousseau's other political writings that show a positive position regarding this question.

12 As we shall see later, Gildin pays some attention to state type 3.

Here, the discussion of the first issue involves my critique of both positivists and negativists; that of the second relates to the refutation of Masters's argument in particular; and that of the third aims to reinforce positivist arguments while rejecting negativist ones. Thus, although my respective arguments about these issues may turn out to be insufficient alone, I hope that they may cumulatively produce an outcome sufficient to refute the negativist interpretation and strengthen the positivist one as a whole.

Are Rousseau's Citizens Not Allowed Public Discussion and Debate in General?

Let us examine the first issue. My interpretation is that although Rousseau issues many critical remarks about public discussion and debate in *The Social Contract*, he nevertheless does not reject them across the board. I shall attempt to develop my argument in relation to the types of state I have presented up to now.

In the case of the ideal peasant state, all the peasant-citizens pass any law submitted by an individual peasant unanimously and without additional public discussion or debate. More accurately speaking, they pass the law without feeling the necessity to engage in these discursive activities. It is better to interpret such a situation as one that does not need public discussion or debate to start with, rather than one that rules them out. This is because peasants are in tune with one another and their hearts are in accord. In the case of the severely corrupted state, at the other extreme, most citizens express opinions spurred by secret and private interests, so that public discussion and debate are useless and even obstructive when it comes to determining the public good. In such a state, the general will becomes mute, for it is not found in majority decisions, and there is therefore no freedom among citizens (IV, i, 109; IV, ii, 111). In this regard, negativist interpretations that focus on state types 1 and 4 to argue that Rousseau rejects public discussion and debate from civic political participation gain much plausibility.

What is left to examine, then, is whether civic participation includes active public interaction in state types 2 and 3–a question that both negative and positive arguments tend to overlook. It is reasonable to suppose that Rousseau intends to apply his political theories in *The Social Contract* not only to the ideal peasant state but also to the semi-ideal and considerably corrupt states, both of which may need his political theory more than the former. Thus, although Rousseau describes public interaction among citizens in a considerably corrupt state in negative terms, using such words as "long debates," "dissensions," "tumult," and "contradictions and debates," it must still be noted that he explicitly acknowledges the probability that the best proposal will be made into law, despite being confronted by disputes (IV, i, 108). Noting this point, Gildin also states: "It is important to note that Rousseau does not despair of the effectiveness of the general will under these circumstances" (Gildin 1983, 151). Thus, in a type 3 state, public interaction seems necessary in order to sift the general will from particular wills, or the best proposal from inadequate proposals. The remaining question, then, is whether public interaction is allowed in Rousseau's semi-ideal state. My intention, however, is to deal with this while examining the second issue: that of how to interpret P1 and P2 consistently. This is because my interpretation of

P1 is closely intertwined with the question whether public interaction is allowed in Rousseau's semi-ideal state.

Finally, in order to complete our investigation of the first issue, we need to examine Manin's apparently powerful argument that *deliberation* in Rousseau's political thought always means choices and decisions reached finally and does not include the process of decision-making. Of course, the examples Manin cites of *deliberation* meaning *decision* seem to secure plausibility. There are other passages in *The Social Contract*, however, in which *deliberation* seems to include interactive discussion and debate; Manin ignores them. In this sense, his examples are selective and not exhaustive. For example, when Rousseau describes the return of unanimity in a completely corrupt state, he uses the word *deliberation* in my interactive sense:

> At the other extreme, unanimity returns. . . . Then fear and flattery turn voting into acclamations. Men no longer deliberate: they adore or they curse. Such was the abject manner in which the senate expressed its opinions under the emperors. (IV, ii, 110)

In this quote, Rousseau contrasts "deliberation" with "adore" and "curse," all of which refer to the process or "manner" by which citizens express their opinions in a public assembly, not to the decision itself, even suggesting that there is a heated debate before voting.

If this passage is insufficient in number or ambiguous in meaning, I may cite another passage in *The Social Contract*:

> because in this institution everyone necessarily subjects

> himself to the conditions he imposes on others, an admirable agreement between interest and justice which confers on common deliberations a quality of equity which vanishes in the discussion of private matters. (II, iv, 63)

At first, here, it appears rather unclear whether the "quality of equity" that is to be conferred on common deliberation refers to the decision or the process, but if we consider the following relative clause, "which vanishes in the discussion of private matters," then "a quality of equity" seems to refer to the process of public interaction rather than the decision itself. We may also note that "a quality of equity" disappears "in the discussion" of private matters–that is, in the process, not in the outcome of the discussion.

If we are allowed to refer to Rousseau's other political writings, we find cases where *deliberation* explicitly refers to the process of interactive participation, notably in *Considerations*: "It is better, in my opinion, to have a less numerous council, and give its members greater freedom, than to increase its size and hamper its freedom of deliberation" (Rousseau 1986, *Considerations*, 200) In short, judging from these quotations, Manin's argument that Rousseau's use of *deliberation* always refers to choices and decisions, not the process of reaching them, turns out to be only partially valid at best and misleading at worst.

How to Render a Consistent Interpretation of P1 and P2

As examined above, McAdam, Masters, and Manin claim,

primarily on the basis of P1, that Rousseau's citizens are not generally allowed public interaction. However, I believe that the "no communication" phrase should be interpreted in a limited way. In developing this argument, I will raise two points. First, I intend to interpret this phrase as forbidding private communication that would provide an opportunity to form small parties and collusion, following Gildin. According to this interpretation, Rousseau's "no communication" prohibits secret or private communication on various matters both in and outside the assembly.[13] This means that Rousseau allows, or at least tolerates, public discussion and debate in citizens' assemblies, in the same manner as jurors during their deliberation. Second, though allowing public deliberation, Rousseau takes special pains to regulate the manner and process of it, as he is keenly aware of the negative side effects of public interaction as well as its benefits. At the same time, he adopts measures to prevent the government from abusing its authority to oppress the freedom of citizens to interact in public, as will be discussed later when I address the third issue: the search for passages in Rousseau's other political writings that show a positive position regarding public discussion and debate.

To elaborate on the first point, the communication among citizens that Rousseau seeks to discourage or ban is that which is

13 I believe that, for similar reasons, jurors are prohibited from obtaining information on the cases with which they are concerned from outside sources and from communicating with others during trials, except during the formal procedure of jury deliberation, in the United States. Although Rousseau's citizens' deliberation is legislative, whereas jury deliberation is adjudicative, I still believe that the former requires public interaction more than the latter, as it is concerned with the general affairs binding the political community as a whole, even for an uncertain future.

likely to lend itself to the formation of small parties and private collusion. Here, it should be remembered that Rousseau discusses the negative effects of factions and partial associations immediately following P1. As is well known, Rousseau is strongly opposed to what we understand today as liberal-pluralist democracy or interest-group politics. These associations and factions, Rousseau thinks, encourage the expression of particular wills or private interests by mutual collusion and aggregation, thereby distorting the public judgment of individual citizens. It is quite clear that Rousseau takes a negative view of secret or private communication among citizens that is likely to lead to the formation of partial associations and private conspiracies.

According to Rousseau, when factions and eloquent speeches prevail in the public assembly, citizens tend to expend their time and energy "adoring" their own faction and "cursing" opposing ones, rather than "deliberating" soberly, so that "long debates, dissensions, and tumult" take over the assembly. We should thus interpret Rousseau as criticizing discussions, debates, and dissensions only insofar as they are colored by private interests and clothed in rhetorical eloquence. Therefore, the context of public deliberation (whether it takes place in a healthy or a corrupt state), its guiding principle (whether citizens seek to find the common good or merely to achieve private interests), and the manner of public expression (whether the public speeches are made by rhetorical eloquence or by simple and plain words) are, for Rousseau, the crucial criteria in deciding whether a given public interaction is worthwhile.

Thus, if we accept the interpretation according to which Rousseau is not opposed to communication among citizens in and of itself–insofar as the corruption of the state has not reached a severe level, civic deliberation is shaped overall by the common good and guided by the general will, and the public expression of citizens' opinions is made in simple and clear speeches–we may interpret the apparently baffling "no communication" phrase as being meant to prohibit secret or private communication among citizens that is liable to lead to the formation of factions and collusion, which in turn hinders the expression of the general will and the pursuit of the common good. This is why Rousseau has to add the following phrase immediately after discussing deleterious effects of factions: "In order for the general will to be well expressed, it is therefore important that there be no partial society in the State, and that each citizen give only his own opinion" (II, iii, 61).

We must now address the second point. My interpretation to the effect that Rousseau seeks to regulate civic public deliberation through government intervention is helpful in understanding P2. In P2, although Rousseau stresses that the right to vote cannot be taken away from citizens, he mentions that the "government is always very careful to allow only to its members" the "right to give an opinion, to make propositions, to analyze, to discuss." However, as we have also seen, he adds a strong qualification by saying that he "could make many comments" on this matter, even to "require a separate treatise," a task that he has to postpone until after *The Social Contract.* Some scholars have been perplexed by this passage's suggestion that the executive exercises powerful influence in the legislative process, with the role of citizens relegated to the mere passive task of voting (Fralin 1978, 525-26). In this regard, the power of the Rousseauean citizens' assembly seems much weaker than those of the Athenian assembly and the Roman comitia, which even enjoyed the right to initiate legislation as well as the right to public deliberation. However, it seems clear that Rousseau's passage does not exclude citizens' right to public interaction. My interpretation is that the lingering note with which Rousseau concludes the sentence in P2 suggests strongly that he agonized over how to strike a balance between the government's need to regulate "long debates, dissensions, and tumult" and its possible abuse of such regulatory power to suppress lively public deliberation among citizens, a point on which I shall soon elaborate further.

Before we examine this, however, we need to turn to the hitherto unaddressed issue of whether Rousseau allows public discussion and debate in his semi-ideal state. In order to discuss this, it should be remembered that my construction of the semi-ideal state is derived from my interpretation of the chapter on the fallibility of the general will (II, iii) and Rousseau's discussion of the Roman comitia (IV, ii). I will thus raise two points, one theoretical and the other historical, to demonstrate that active public interaction is necessary in order to find the general will and to turn it into law in the semi-ideal state.

The theoretical point is concerned with how to find the general will through majority rule. As we have seen, the general will is still expressed more often in the semi-ideal state than in the considerably corrupt state, but it is obtained by majoritarian or supermajoritarian rule rather than by the unanimity of the ideal state. Rousseau suggests how to derive the general will from the will of all in the semi-ideal state in a well-known metaphorical passage just before P1: "But take away from these same wills [a sum of private wills, or the will of all] the pluses and minuses that cancel each other out, and the remaining sum of the differences is the general will" (II, iii).[14] In order to obtain this transformative result, Rousseau stresses the necessary presence of the "large number of small differences" in the deliberation of citizens, which is of course one of the main reasons for his opposition to factions and partial associations. It must be noted here that matters in the citizen's assembly are not to be decided simply by a yes or no vote. If this were the case, the simple majority rule would suffice and there would be no need to go through the cumbersome mutual cancellation process. At the same time, the task of interpreting what Rousseau metaphorically coins "pluses and minuses" and canceling them against each other is not one that should be assigned to the government, which tends to abuse its power and oppress the freedom of citizens. The task, moreover, should be carried out before voting, not afterward, which suggests that interactive public deliberation among citizens should take place before voting.[15] If these tasks of interpretation and cancellation were assumed by the government after voting, the government would usurp the citizens' right to vote by arbitrarily manipulating voting outcomes and popular sovereignty would vanish into thin air.

---

14 With regard to this process, see Gildin's illuminating interpretation (Gildin 1983, 55-57).

15 By suggesting additional reasons, this interpretation reinforces that of Schwartzberg, that there should be a discursive process before voting. Interpreting P1, Gildin also suggests that there should be active public deliberation in order to guarantee its "rectitude": "Rousseau obviously assumes that the assembly will include members with the ability to enlighten their fellow citizens" (Gildin 1983, 57-58). He does not, however, provide substantial evidence or argumentation to support this assumption.

My second point is the historical argument that Rousseau takes the early Roman republic as an example of the semi-ideal state, the characteristics of which I have described earlier. In the Roman comitia, as Rousseau describes it, resolutions were passed by "a large majority of votes," for there were no factions formed and no ascendancy of private interests. It seems important to note that Rousseau keeps significant silence about the right of Roman citizens to propose laws and discuss them in his praise of the Roman republic, while being critical of the same practice in corrupt Athens. This means that Rousseau approves of such Roman practices as long as Rome remains healthy on the whole.[16]

Passages Showing Rousseau's Recognition of Public Discussion and Debate

It is now time to address the third issue by locating passages that show Rousseau's explicit admission of active civic public interaction. With regard to this, we may first point to the fact that Rousseau complained strongly to the Genevan government in *Letters* that a Genevan citizen could not "propose anything in these assemblies [general Conseil], one cannot discuss anything in them, one cannot deliberate over anything," owing to regulations imposed by the executive Conseil in the name of public security, while describing past

16 In this context, it is useful to recall Machiavelli's chapter in *Discourses* titled "How Free Government Can Be Maintained in Corrupt Cities, If It Is Already There; and If It Is Not There, How It Can Be Set Up," in which he shows that the good Roman custom of granting citizens the right to propose and discuss laws turned into a harmful practice when people became wicked and corrupt (*Discourses*, book 1, chap. 18, 241-42).

political practice, where citizens were able to speak more freely–even to shout–in a comparatively positive light (Rousseau 2001, 250-51).[17]

We also find, furthermore, that Rousseau explicitly acknowledges public discussion and debate among citizens in his last political writing, *Considerations on the Government of Poland.* When depicting proceedings in the diets and dietines,[18] he stresses that it is more important to ensure freedom than to impose regulation and asserts that the rights of citizens to speak, discuss, and debate, which naturally accompany collective deliberation, be permitted:

> All the measures you adopt to prevent licence in the legislative order, though good in themselves, will sooner or later be used to oppress it. Long and useless harangues, which waste so much time, are a great evil; but it is an even greater evil for a good citizen not to dare speak when he has something useful to say. When it reaches the point where certain mouths only are opened in the diets, and even those are forbidden to speak freely, they soon will say nothing but what is apt to please the powerful. (Rousseau 1986, 198; cf. 196)

As this passage shows, Rousseau stresses the evil of lengthy speeches, but at the same time emphasizes more strongly that they should not be entirely suppressed.

17 Of course, this passage cannot be interpreted as direct evidence that Rousseau allows public discussion and debate, although it is suggestive of this. It also merits our attention, however, in that *deliberation* here refers to active public interaction.

18 Here it should be remembered that dietines refer to regional assemblies in which citizens participate directly, whereas diets are representative assemblies.

In a passage immediately following this quote, Rousseau argues that certain measures regarding the appointment of officials and the distribution of favors should be taken in order to reduce "vain harangues and flatteries," and then that regulation of citizens' manner of speaking should be additionally introduced:

> In order to prune away some of the farragoes of rhetorical nonsense you might, however, require each orator to announce at the beginning of his discourse the proposition he wants to establish and, after presenting his arguments, to summarise his conclusions, as lawyers do in court. If that did not make speeches shorter, it would at least restrain those who merely want to talk for the sake of talking, and waste time to no purpose. (Rousseau 1986, 198)

The two quotes I draw from *Considerations* clearly show that the negative interpretation examined thus far falls short of doing justice to Rousseau's political thought as a consistent whole. They also suggest that Rousseau took continual pains to strike a balance between the governmental need to regulate public proceedings and the danger of the abuse of governmental regulative power, as he is fully aware of the evils of both.

At this point, we would raise a question: To which type of state did Poland belong at the time that Rousseau prescribed a system of government for it? Although Rousseau praised the Polish love of liberty and the Poles' struggle for independence against Russia, Poland did not seem to belong to the semi-ideal state, nor did it belong to the severely corrupt state. The country would thus seem to fit into either the considerably corrupt state category or between the semi-ideal state and the considerably corrupt state. If my reasoning is plausible, it boils down to confirmation of my point that Rousseau was still willing to grant interactive public deliberation in the considerably corrupt state.

Concluding Remarks

As my examination has shown so far, the negativists seem unable to escape the suspicion that they attempt to fit Rousseau's more complicated ideas about civic political participation into their simplified interpretive schemes, by focusing and expanding on certain selected passages in *The Social Contract* and ignoring Rousseau's agony over striking a fine balance between "discipline" and "liberty":

> A better system of discipline in the diets and dietines would surely be most useful: but I can never repeat too often that you must not seek two contradictory things at the same time. Discipline is good, but liberty is better; and the more you hedge in liberty with formalities, the more means of usurpation will these formalities furnish. (Rousseau 1986, 198)

At the same time, the positivists as well as the negativists seem to overlook the point that civic public discussion and debate might well be permitted and useful in state types 2 and 3, located between the two extreme state types 1 and 4, for they derive their general interpretations primarily from passages relevant to the extreme types.

Finally, negativists may well sidestep my critique by arguing that the general principle of Rousseau's political thought is to exclude public discussion and debate from citizen's participation and that passages drawn from *Letters* and *Considerations* constitute only exceptions to this general principle. That is to say, Rousseau's general principles are laid out in *The Social Contract* and some variations are made when he makes actual applications of them in *Letters* and *Considerations*. A similar relationship may be observed between Plato's two major political works, *The Republic* and *The Laws*. Rousseau, however, is not conscious of the kind of discrepancies between principles and exceptions that negativists may point to. On the contrary, he makes clear in many passages that the arguments he puts forward in *Considerations* are consistent with the principles he has articulated in *The Social Contract*. That is, it is the outcome of direct application of his principles (Rousseau 1986, 195, 190).

Rousseau does not approve of public discussion or debate enthusiastically or unconditionally. As has been confirmed repeatedly by my examination, Rousseau favors harmonious decision reached by unanimity or overwhelming majority that is not accompanied by wasteful discussions and exhaustive debates. It may, however, be an unreasonable exaggeration of Rousseau's political thought to jump to the conclusion that he bans in toto public discussion and debate that inevitably accompany civic political participation, thereby reducing the role of citizens to that of simply casting votes. This point is confirmed more explicitly in the passages cited from *Considerations* in which Rousseau still seeks a solution in regulating the right of citizens to speak in the public assembly instead of banning it completely, while remaining critical of "long and useless harangues" and "flatteries."

In light of all the foregoing, my position regarding whether Rousseau's civic political participation allows public discussion and debate is a moderately positive one. If Rousseau attempts, in P1, to suppress communication among citizens that is likely to lead to collusion and the formation of small associations, he also seeks, in P2 and passages we have drawn from *Letters* and *Considerations*, to positively accommodate public civic discussion and debate. In the latter case, although he is willing to propose governmental power to intervene in public proceedings in order to prevent the civic right to free speech from getting out of control through its abuse by a powerful few, he also issues a strong warning of the dangers of oppressing civic liberty. In short, my interpretation is the elaboration and clarification of Gildin's rather vague yet flexible interpretation that "Rousseau's remarks suggest that there are many possible arrangements regarding the right to propose and to debate laws compatible with his principles."

References

Crocker, Lester G. 1967. "Introduction." In *The Social Contract and Discourse on the Origin of Inequality*, edited by Lester G. Crocker, vii-xxiv. New York: Washington Square Press.

Fralin, Richard. 1978. "The Evolution of Rousseau's View of Representative Government." *Political Theory* 6 (4): 517-36.

Gildin, Hilail. 1983. *Rousseau's Social Contract: The Design of Argument.* Chicago: University of Chicago Press.

Habermas, Jürgen. 1989. *The Structural Transformation of the Public Sphere.* Translated by Thomas Burger. Cambridge, MA: MIT Press.

McAdam, James. 1967. "What Rousseau Meant by the General Will." *Dialogue* 5 (4): 498-515.

Machiavelli, Niccolò. 1965. *Discourses.* In *Machiavelli: The Chief Works and Others*, vol 1. Edited and translated by Allan Gilbert. Durham, NC: Duke University Press.

Manin, Bernard. 1987. "On Legitimacy and Political Deliberation." *Political Theory* 15 (3): 338-68.

Masters, Roger D. 1968. *The Political Philosophy of Rousseau.* Princeton, NJ: Princeton University Press.

Rousseau, Jean-Jacques. 1964. *Du Contrat Social–Écrits Politiques.* Vol. III of *Oeuvres Complètes*, edited by Bernard Gagnebin and Marcel Raymond. Paris: Editions Gallimard.

——. 1978. *On the Social Contract with Geneva Manuscript and Political Economy.* Edited by Roger D. Masters. Translated by Judith R. Masters. New York: St. Martin's Press.

——. 1986. *Considerations on the Government of Poland* in *Political Writings*, translated and edited by Frederick Watkins, 159-274. Madison: University of Wisconsin Press.

——. 2001. *The Collected Writings of Rousseau*. Vol 9. Translated by Christopher Kelly and Judith R. Bush. Edited by Christopher Kelly and Eve Grace. Hanover, NH: University Press of New England.

Schwartzberg, Melissa. 2008. "Voting the General Will: Rousseau on Decision Rules." *Political Theory* 36 (3): 403-23.

Chapter 7

Politics and Truth: An Analysis of Richard E. Kim's Novel *The Martyred*

In his novel *The Martyred*, Richard E. Kim, a Korean-American novelist, raises fascinating questions with regard to politics and truth: (1) Is it possible to uphold Christian truth in the contemporary condition? And (2) is it desirable to reveal the ugly truth to the masses regardless of its possible impact upon our political community? Whereas the first question is concerned with religious, transcendental truth, the second takes issue with factual truth. These two questions are intertwined in such a complex and intricate way in the novel that it is difficult to unravel them in a compelling way. The purpose of this chapter is to analyze the relationship between politics and truth in terms of these two issues, which are addressed throughout the novel. From these issues arise a series of additional important questions. What has been the relation of truth to politics in the Western political tradition? What is the status of truth in the contemporary political world? What is the value of truth for the political community? How has the conflict between politics and truth been manifested and resolved? Why do our political leaders have to deceive people in their name? What kind of contribution does deception make, in its best form, to our political community? How can we confirm the sincere motives that underlie the deceptions of our political leaders? I may not be able to discuss all these questions fully in this chapter, but I will attempt to examine them insofar as they illuminate Kim's novel *The Martyred*. Though my purpose is not to provide answers to all of them, I would be satisfied if my serious engagement with them through analysis of *The Martyred* enhances the quality of the questions for thoughtful readers.

A Brief Summary of *The Martyred*

Before entering into this analysis, a brief summary of *The Martyred* seems mandatory for those who have not read it. The basic question, the magnetic center of the novel, is whether it is desirable to reveal the truth about twelve ministers who were executed by North Korean communists on the day the June 25 War (the Korean War) started. Fourteen prominent ministers in North Korea had been arrested by the communists a week before the war broke out. After the United Nations (UN) forces and the South Korean army captured Pyongyang [Pyeongyang], the capital city of North Korea, South Korean army intelligence started an investigation of the missing ministers with the motivation to exhibit to the entire world a grave case of religious persecution by the communists. That is to say, it was initiated with the political purpose of revealing communist atrocities and inhumanities.

But as the investigation was to ultimately show, the twelve martyrs did not die saintly and heroic deaths, contrary to initial assumptions. According to Major Jung, a North Korean communist involved in the execution who was later captured by South Korean army intelligence, these so-called great heroes and martyrs died like dogs, denouncing their God and one another and submitting to the torture and interrogation of the communists. Only two ministers, Mr. Hann and Mr. Shin, escaped execution. Mr. Hann was the protégé of Reverend Park, the leader of the group of ministers. Reverend Park was among the twelve who were executed; however, he refused to pray to an unjust God just before the execution when some of the ministers asked him to pray for them. When Hann saw Park betraying his God and later heard from Shin about the secret of his faith–atheism–Hann collapsed in devastated despair and lost his mind. This is the primary reason "the Reds" spared his life. But Shin put up a good fight, never submitting to the Reds' torture, and was spared the executioners' bullets out of their admiration for his courage.

Here arises a problem. For, despite the surprising discovery of the unheroic deaths of the twelve ministers, the military authority (represented by Colonel Chang) did not flinch from the original plan for the joint memorial service for the martyrs, but continued to carry it out. Main characters in the novel were thus divided into opposing camps: Colonel Chang, the chief of Army Political Intelligence, was the primary proponent and the government's executor of the service. He thought that, in the end, both Christians and the military fought the communists. He liked to use the twelve martyrs as a symbol of suffering Christians and their eventual triumph over the Reds. He sought to use them as tools of political propaganda, having little interest in their martyrdom itself. To the surprise of all the characters, Shin would ultimately approve of the joint memorial service and willingly cooperate in the plan. Chaplain Koh, Captain Lee (an Army Political Intelligence officer and narrator of the novel), and Captain Park (son of Reverend Park) were vehemently opposed to the plan, asserting that religious martyrdom could not be manufactured by political fiat. But later, both Park and Koh, deeply moved by Shin's exemplary actions and sermons, changed their minds and joined the memorial service. Captain Lee alone remained the most adamant opponent of the plan, advocating that the truth should be revealed regardless of its consequences.

After the announcement of the joint (military and religious) memorial service for the martyrs was made, the martyrdom of the twelve ministers became a fait accompli and the presence of Shin at the scene of the execution became known to the public. As a consequence, Shin's fortunate survival became an object of growing suspicion by the Christians. Then angry Christian crowds rushed to his house and mocked him, surrounding it and chanting "Judas!" Therefore, he withdrew at once to another local city and declared that he would resign from his ministry. But as he continued to witness the suffering and misery of people in the countryside during his retreat, he changed his mind and decided to join the memorial service. In that service and a series of subsequent revival services, he glorified the twelve martyrs and humiliated himself as a sinner who had not been strong enough to endure the torture and follow their example.

Shin, Chang, and Captain Park die at the end of the novel. After Chinese intervention in the war, the UN and South Korean armies retreated from Pyongyang. Shin refused to leave Pyongyang, despite Lee's repeated admonitions to do so. Thus, he was arrested and thrown in jail after the Chinese arrived. But there were conflicting rumors about his last days. Some said that he was executed in Pyongyang, whereas the majority of North Korean refugees said they had seen him almost everywhere in North Korea. Colonel Chang, too, died a heroic death. He sacrificed himself to save his raiding party and went beyond the call of duty during a secret operation in North Korea. Park was severely wounded on the front lines and died in a hospital. Chaplain Koh, after being discharged from military service, opened a church in Pusan [Busan] for North Korean refugees. Lee, the most adamant truth-teller throughout the novel, went outside after a visit to Koh's church to attend his service and, while watching the night sky, experienced a mysterious feeling of re-enchantment with the universe, similar to the way Meursault did in Camus's *The Stranger*.[1]

Even if I tried to make this short summary more intelligible, ambiguity and haziness would still remain about the genuine circumstances under which the twelve were murdered and the two survived. This may show Kim's literary genius. The truth about the twelve martyrs was gradually revealed, albeit in a fragmentary form. How the fourteen ministers conducted themselves in the face of torture and execution was never clearly revealed. What a reader can

1 Actually, Richard Kim dedicated his novel to Albert Camus, "whose insight into 'a strange form of love' overcame for me the nihilism of the trenches and bunkers of Korea."

do to comprehend the whole situation is to patch together fragments of the truth, which are unveiled in conversations between the main characters–in the form of subjective opinions, memories, and political propaganda–rather than through detached objective observation. This shows how fragile and perishable factual truth really is and how much it depends upon human memory, as I shall discuss later.

As a novelist, Kim describes the mysterious nature of truth in a literary form (i.e., symbolically in the form of a clanging bell, the bell tower, and various characters' attitudes toward them). The bell tower was located in Reverend Park's church, the Central Presbyterian Church, which was almost completely destroyed by bombing. It brings different meanings and messages to the characters in the novel, depending upon their position toward the truth. The lonely clanging of the bell sounded mysterious and revelatory about the martyred to Captain Lee, who was curious about it as a truth-seeker. The clanging of the bell invoked a sense of religious awe and worship to ordinary people who did not know the truth about the martyred. Also, a man, during his conversation with Lee, unwittingly suggested the symbolic relationship between the bell tower and the truth about the twelve martyrs, saying "Nobody touches it [the bell]. The wind comes and rings the bell. . . . You can't get up there [to the bell tower]. The stairway is almost gone, and it's too dangerous to use a ladder. The tower may crumble at any moment" (Kim 1964, 24).

However, the clanging of the bell sounded intolerably irritating to Colonel Chang, who tried to present the twelve ministers as religious martyrs by any means necessary in order to use them for political propaganda. Hann, the crazy young minister, visited this place to pray, a scene that would remind us of the fact that his mentor, the Reverend Park, had refused to pray in his final moments. Later, when the twelve martyrs became known to the public, the Central Presbyterian Church became a pilgrimage site for Christians. But when the Chinese and the North Korean communists took over Pyongyang, it was completely destroyed. Moreover, the contrast between Mr. Shin's church, which had been preserved almost intact, and Reverend Park's church, which had been all but destroyed, seemed to symbolize the differences between Park and Shin in their faith and fate. Thus, in a literary and symbolic form, Kim describes the predicament of religious and factual truths in the contemporary world, the topic to which I now turn.

Truth and the Modern Predicament

Before we analyze the relationship of truth to politics, I would like to divide truth into three categories: rational, religious/philosophical, and factual.[2] Hannah Arendt makes a distinction between rational and factual truths in her famous essay "Truth and Politics." But I would like to add one more category of truth, religious/philosophical truth, for the purpose of this chapter. According to Arendt, rational truth includes mathematical, scientific, and philosophical truths. For example, Euclidean mathematics, Einstein's theory of relativity, and Plato's doctrine of ideas belong to

2 I shall use this distinction for the sake of convenience without examining its intrinsic legitimacy, insofar as it is useful to my analysis in this chapter.

the category of rational truth. For Arendt, rational truth can be arrived at by solid reasoning and experiment. Factual truth is concerned with everyday events, historical facts, and our opinions, all of which are dependent upon memory, either collective or personal (Arendt 1977, 231).[3] Finally, religious/philosophical truth is disclosed or known to humans by philosophical speculation and divine revelation. Although Arendt classifies philosophical truths as part of rational truth, it seems to me that most philosophical truths form another independent category. For although some philosophical truths may approach "rational" truth, most of these–for example, one might recall Plato's doctrine of ideas, social contract theory, or natural law doctrine–and so-called religious truths cannot be verified by solid reasoning and experiment. Thus, they rather belong to an independent category that might also be called transcendental or metaphysical truths.

If we consider the relationships of the three kinds of truths to political power, we find that political power cannot do away with rational and philosophical/religious truths such as Newtonian physics, Plato's doctrine of ideas, or the Christian doctrine of salvation. Yet factual truth is less able to survive the distortions made by political power. According to Arendt, "Facts and events are infinitely more fragile things than axioms, discoveries, theories–even the most widely speculative ones–produced by the human mind: they occur in the field of the ever-changing affairs of men . . . " (Arendt 1977, 231). Thus, she notes, "The chances of factual truth surviving the

3 Thus, Arendt attributes the origin of Western historiography to humans' attempt to keep factual truth–the spoken words, all the actions and deeds that go on between mortals directly–from vanishing from our mortal memories (Arendt 1977, 41-43).

onslaught of power, therefore, are very slim; it is always in danger of being maneuvered out of the world not only for a time but, potentially, forever" (Arendt 1977, 231). Once facts and events are lost, no rational effort will bring them back. Of course, the chances of recovering rational truths, in case they are lost, may not be good, either. Yet they have far better chances of recovery than do factual truths, for the former are rational and depend upon solid reasoning, whereas the latter are contingent in nature and depend upon ever-shifting memories for their existence (Arendt, 1977, 231-32).

In the modern age, although rational truth has been widely welcomed and respected with the impressive development of modern sciences and technologies, transcendental and factual truths have been confronted with unprecedented difficulties. Then what is the modern predicament of truths, both transcendental and factual? In the premodern age, humans believed that their universe was created, ordered, and guarded by God (a transcendental Being) and that political society was embedded in that universe. They placed themselves at the center of the universe as a partaker in a stable, divine order. In other words, they thought that if only they could pattern their political society after metaphysical principles such as Platonic ideas, the *tao/dao* (道), the Mandate of Heaven (天命), the law of nature, absolute reason, and other transcendental truths, they would secure a stable and harmonious political order that had been found to always be in constant flux and subject to ever-shifting change. For premodern humans, such metaphysical truths meant discovery of a pre-established order that independently existed outside humans. Given that they held the notion that "man's cognitive apparatus did not itself basically condition the quality and nature of what was known, . . . discoveries made by the methods of science, philosophy, and theology were not fabrications of the human mind, but faithful reflections or representations of an order independent of the discoverer" (Schaar 1981, 28).

But the unprecedented growth of secularism, science, and technology since the nineteenth century has unmasked and eclipsed all illusions about ourselves, metaphysical truths, and any transcendental order. It has exposed us and the world we inhabit to stark nakedness. Copernicus, Darwin, Marx, Nietzsche, Freud, and Einstein have also led us to entertain a profound distrust of all religions, ideologies, and other metaphysical absolute standards. All truths, including even scientific ones, are no longer "discovered" and are not free from the suspicion of fabrication by the human mind. Today, hardly anybody takes such metaphysical or transcendental truths seriously enough to stake his or her life on or to interfere with worldly affairs.[4] Rather, the poignancy of the modern predicament lies in the paradox that human experiences suddenly become divested of their stable meaning and become chaotic as a result of the loss of our belief in metaphysical truths that used to provide stable settings and standards for our actions. Despite our craving for order and transcendent meaning, we have to accept that the world has no absolute God-given meaning. After all, our world itself is dependent upon our fragile practices

4 Therefore, we might say that the age-old conflict between philosophy and politics, between two opposing ways of life that had persisted since the beginning of Western political philosophy, has been resolved by the sheer impotence and irrelevance of metaphysical truths as the guide for human action (Arendt 1977, 232-36).

and conventions (Pitkin 1972, 316-19). This predicament of the transcendental truth in a post-Nietzschean, godless world is presented vividly in *The Martyred* as well, as I shall examine later.

On the contrary, the tension between political power and factual truth has been on the rise in the contemporary world. Deliberate lying about factual truth by political leaders is not new to modern society. Their lies, however, were made regarding particular facts and toward their enemy (Arendt 1977, 253). But the notable trend in lying about the factual truth with the advent of mass society is, as Arendt points out, the prevalence of "organized lying," "defactualization," "rewriting contemporary history," and "image-making of all sorts" by political power (Arendt 1977, 251-52). Modern political lies deal with "things that are not secrets at all but are known to practically everybody" (Arendt 1977, 252). In short, they are made for domestic consumption. All these lies are intended as full-fledged substitutes for reality, through constant indoctrination and mass propaganda. It is the development of modern communications technology and the mass media that makes possible such systematic destruction of factual truths, the very texture of our lives. Such need for massive political lies is particularly strong during wars or revolutionary struggles for the purpose of attracting mass support or deluding people. *The Martyred* deals with the precarious fate of factual truth at the hands of modern political power in a Korean context; that is, during the June 25 War.

The Tension between Politics and Transcendental Truth in *The Martyred*

The tension between unjust politics that plague the world and transcendental (Christian) truth permeates *The Martyred*. Indeed, this main theme of the novel constitutes its dynamic tension. All the main characters fell in sheer disarray witnessing the horror and injustice, hunger and sickness, and sudden, meaningless death that the war brought to the Korean people. Whether they were Christian or not, they were struggling with the questions, "Why must there be so much injustice and misery in the world? Why must we suffer?" as Captain Park put it (Kim 1964, 227). Mr. Shin was also deeply agonized by the injustice plaguing his country. Thus, the Christian truth (i.e., we have to suffer to prove our faith in God) was on serious trial during the war, confronted with the stark injustice suffered by the Korean people. Thus, when Lee asked on their first meeting, "your God–is he aware of the suffering of his people?" Shin could not answer (Kim 1964, 37).

Furthermore, Shin simply attributed his survival to "divine intervention" and then had to immediately amend that, saying, "Then call it luck," if Lee did not believe in God (Kim 1964, 33-34). On another occasion Shin told Lee that his fortunate survival was a "near-miracle," but he conceded that "miracle is a difficult word to understand these days" (Kim 1964, 55). What makes a certain event a miracle in the eyes of Christians is their faith–"Faith will move a mountain." So he implicitly suggested that his faith was not solid. He may have even been scornful of his survival. In his later encounter with Lee, Shin finally confessed the secret of his faith: "All my life I have searched for God, Captain, but I found only man with all his sufferings . . . death, inexorable death! . . . Nothing! Nothing!" (Kim 1964, 256). Thus, beneath the immeasurable serenity he maintained in appearance lay a terrible agony tormenting him.

Mr. Shin had actually revealed his un-Christian faith to his wife and Hann before, albeit to disastrous effect. He once resented his wife's slavish devotion to God and her pitiful prayers, when after the death of their child she blamed the loss on her sins, spending all her time praying and fasting. Thus, he told her that they would never see their child again and that there would be, indeed, no afterlife. She could not bear his horrible remark and died in despair. Despite his pledge never to reveal his secret, however, he again revealed his doubts about God to Hann, again with disastrous results. After making two fatal blunders, it was natural that he should decide never to disclose his personal doubts.

While continuously praying to God, Shin seemed to despair that God's truth seemed irrelevant to justice in the world; that is, sufferings here and now. If the injustices plaguing the world were not connected to the ultimate and eternal justice (truth) of God through our unshakable faith, then the sufferings of this world lose much of their meaning. In other words, Shin was suffering from what Max Weber has called the "age-old problem of theodicy"; that is, "the very question of how it is that a power which is said to be at once omnipotent and kind could have created such an irrational world of undeserved suffering, unpunished injustice, and hopeless stupidity" (Weber 1958, 122). Thus, Shin was possessed of a fundamental skepticism about the inscrutability of God's justice. Out of despair, he had lost his faith and ceased to believe in God, as he confessed to Lee.

However, the fact that Mr. Shin remained a minister despite his skepticism and doubt about God, shows that he acted like Camus's Sisyphus. In *The Myth of Sisyphus*, Camus tries to overcome the modern predicament of the world of godlessness and to reinstate the dignity of humankind by assuming an attitude both absurd and heroic:

> If the myth is tragic, that is because its hero is conscious. . . . Sisyphus, proletarian of the gods, powerless and rebellious, knows the whole extent of his wretched condition: it is what he thinks of during his descent. The lucidity that was to constitute his torture at the same time crowns his victory. There is no fate that cannot be surmounted by scorn. (Camus 1955, 119-21)

Camus's Sisyphus represents mortals' tragic awareness of universal pain in life. His Sisyphus conquers an unintelligible and cruel fate by consciously scorning it. Camus even goes so far as to cry, "One must imagine Sisyphus happy" (Camus 1955, 123). He also provides Sisyphus with the unequivocal strength to stand alone.

Then, are the masses capable of bearing this enormous burden of absurd truth–the tragic awareness of the universal pain and suffering in life–and standing alone? Should Shin let the masses face such a universe, one torn apart by a meaningless internecine war and a maddening ideological confrontation, without illusions? On this issue, Shin, Koh, and Chang parted company with Captain Lee. When he returned to Pyongyang from the countryside and joined the joint memorial service, resuming his ministry, Shin had already decided to actively lie to his congregation in order to give them the illusion of eternal hope–that there is an eternal kingdom of God and ultimate justice. Now his main concern was switched from God's eternal life to the life here and now (i.e., his people's survival during a devastating war). The salvation of human souls by God became a greatly irrelevant scheme to Shin. Thus, in his case, the tension between humans' craving for justice here and now and the Christian truth that one must suffer to prove one's faith in God was resolved only by giving humans the illusion of eternal justice, instead of telling the horrible truth of his atheism.

In contrast, Lee stubbornly insisted that the ugly factual truth about the twelve murdered ministers, which might ultimately undermine Christian faith in God, be exposed to the public, regardless of the impact such exposure would have upon the masses and Christianity itself. Lee was also suffering from the naked brutality of the war, whose purpose he could never justify. He was questioning the justice of God, horrified by the meaningless, devastating war. But he was enduring the sufferings without relying upon the illusion of an afterlife or transcendental truth. Therefore, he insisted that all human beings, without exception and exemption, must equally learn to live with and face a godless world and meaningless life. He wanted to believe that the masses were capable of doing so. He was quite suspicious and critical of all pretensions, noble lies, and myth which, cloaking harsh reality, made life appear softer, tolerable, and even meaningful. He might have argued that it was this pleasing illusion that justified and perpetuated human suffering, misery, and self-deception. The first step to put an end to them, he would assert, was to liberate the masses from such illusions and pretensions.

Basically, Lee argues that all people must act like Camus's Sisyphus. In making such arguments, however, Lee does not consider the frailties and weakness of human beings or their differing capacities to meet such heroic tasks. His assertion does not take concrete situations into consideration. Whenever he was asked what he would do if he were in others' situation, he merely said, "Truth must be told." There is no reference to concrete human actors in the flesh or particular circumstances in his assertion. Thus, Lee's uncompromising attitude was made clear in Captain Park's accusation: "You only say you understand them. You view their sufferings and their despair in a detached, intellectual way precisely because you are merely a sympathetic observer" (Kim 1964, 159). Lee tries to keep himself moralistic by leaving himself out of the picture. His attitude, when introduced to the public realm, may become apolitical or antipolitical.

Shin would agree with Lee on all points but one: The masses are not capable of facing the truth without illusions or standing alone like Sisyphus; only a few such as Lee and himself are so able. As I discussed earlier, Shin's experiences of having revealed his atheism to his wife and Hann were traumatic. He found that they were not able to withstand the absurdity of suffering. When Lee exasperatedly insisted that Shin tell the truth about the twelve ministers to the people, he only said suggestively, "My young friend, has it ever occurred to you that they may not want the truth?" (Kim 1964, 103). Instead of telling the truth, therefore, he decided to actively lie to the people to give them some hope and to prevent them from falling into bottomless despair.[5]

Thus, whereas divine justice turns out to be highly inscrutable at best and seriously doubtful at worst, we may find the principle of existential justice still working in Shin's selfless devotion to the suffering masses. In order to understand this, it seems useful to note what Tarrou, the narrator in Camus's *The Plague*, says to Dr. Rieux, the hero:

> That's why I say there are pestilences and there are victims; no more than that. . . . I grant we should add a third category: that of true healers. But it's a fact one doesn't come across many of them, and anyhow it must be a hard vocation. That's why I decided to take, in every predicament, the victims' side, so as to reduce the damage done. Among them I can at least try to discover how one attains to the third category; in other words, to peace. (Camus 1947, 230)

Mr. Shin in *The Martyred* is actually Dr. Rieux of *The Plague* in minister's dress. For both Shin and Rieux, the role of justice is, therefore, relegated from the once-crowning principle of our political community–distribution of reward and punishment to the members of the community in accordance with their achievement or dereliction–to a more modest status of sharing and reducing the suffering of mortals.

5 Shin's remark, "That [his own despair] is my cross" in his reply to Lee's question, "What about your despair?" is reminiscent of Camus's Sisyphus as well (Kim 1964, 256-57).

Deception as a Symbolic Use of Politics: Lying in Politics

In *The Prince*, while debunking Platonic utopianism, Machiavelli scornfully stresses that "a man who neglects what is actually done for what should be done learns the way to self-destruction rather than self-preservation" (Machiavelli 1981, 91). Therefore, in order to maintain his rule, Machiavelli says, a prince "must learn how not to be virtuous, and to make use of this or not according to need" (Machiavelli 1981, 91).[6] As a consequence, Machiavelli even twists the meaning of the word *virtue*. His concept of virtue (virtù) is totally separated from the Christian or Cicero's meaning of *virtue*. He uses the word *virtue* to mean something akin to manliness, energetic strength, military valor, or prudence. Thus, his prince must not mind carrying out some cruelties, being miserly, or not honoring his word, whenever conditions dictate.

But the prince should know how to escape the evil reputation attached to those vices, as well as the hatred and derision of the populace. For Machiavelli, such a reputation is more likely to lose him his state. Therefore, he claims that the prince has to maintain the appearance of good as much as possible, while not refraining from committing those vices necessary for the safeguarding of the state. He even says, "He [the prince] should appear to be compassionate, faithful to his word, kind, guileless, and devout" (Machiavelli 1981, 100). Because everyone "sees what you appear to be [and]

6 Machiavelli's insight into the prince is also applicable to Christian leaders, including the Pope, as well as political leaders in contemporary mass society.

few experience what you really are," appearance is more important in maintaining the good will of the people (Machiavelli 1981, 101). The gist of Machiavelli's argument is that the prince should be hypocritical. As goes the old saying, "Hypocrisy is the tribute vice pays to virtue," hypocrisy has a stabilizing effect upon society by confirming and reinforcing the mainstream values of a society so that it is less dangerous to society than a Socratic kind of direct challenge to the prevailing norms. Hypocrisy acknowledges the ethical superiority of virtue over vice, just as blasphemy confirms the existence of God rather than denying it. Therefore, even though the action of a prince is liberated from the regulation of moral precepts, it is restrained by his constant need to maintain the appearance of good.

As Plato points out, appearance resides in the realm of opinion, which is always shifting, temporary, and capricious. Since maintaining a good appearance depends upon the opinion of the people who watch from a distance, the prince, while trying to disguise his actions under the guise of looking good, has to pay vigilant attention to what the public thinks of him. This can still be an enormous burden to the prince, because he is torn between Machiavelli's dictum that he must be willing to commit those vices necessary to the safeguarding of the state and the other precept that he must appear to possess all the virtues people praise (Machiavelli 1981, 92, 100).

But Machiavelli does not think it too difficult to maintain the appearance of good. In his discussion of cruelty and compassion, he says, "By making an example or two he [the prince] will prove [himself] more compassionate than those who, being too compassionate, allow disorders which lead to murder and rapine"

(Machiavelli 1981, 95). Here, he recognizes the symbolic dimension of politics. Political analysis is not only concerned with how political actions bring tangible rewards to some groups–"Who gets what and how?"–but also with how these same actions placate or arouse the mass public (Edelman 1985, 12). Political acts are not only instrumental, but also symbolic.

Thus we can make an interesting observation about the relationship among "what ought to be," "what is," and "what seems" in Machiavelli's thought. Whereas he is willing to prescribe anything for the sake of his prince being able to seize and maintain power according to the dictate of what is, he is keenly aware of what the populace wants and what the moral precepts demand from his prince. He makes the strongest case ever for the separation and autonomy of politics ("what is") from ethics ("what ought to be"). Yet he does not ignore the ethical dimension of politics, as we are liable to assume. He has his own way of meeting moral precepts by manipulating what the prince seems to be. What seems to be–the prince's symbolic action–would satisfy what ought to be. In short, for Machiavelli, the form (or the symbolic dimension) of political action, which consists of maintaining an appearance of good and using manipulative symbols, would satisfy what ought to be, whereas its substance is designed to meet what is or what circumstances dictate.

Drawing upon Murray Edelman, let me briefly elaborate on the theme of politics as symbolic action in contemporary mass society in order to shed light on Mr. Shin's action. Politics distributes goods, services, and power to specific political actors or groups. But it also conveys symbols that large masses of humans need to believe about the state to reassure themselves. According to Edelman, basic to the recognition of the symbolic dimension of politics is a "distinction between politics as a spectator sport and political activity utilized by organized groups to get quite specific, tangible benefits for themselves." However, for most humans most of the time, "politics is a series of pictures in the mind, placed there by television news, newspapers, magazines, and discussion" (Edelman 1985, 5). In other words, politics is for most of us like a passing parade of abstract symbols such as the images and shadows of the Platonic cave. In these activities, we are not able to check our acts and assumptions against the consequences and subsequently correct errors. There is no feedback, unlike in our everyday routine activities. Thus, Edelman stresses that the symbolic dimension of politics becomes all the more crucial in a contemporary society in which humans are alienated from politics, because politics "is remote, set apart, but omnipresent as the ultimate threat or means of succor, yet not susceptible to effective influence through any act as we individuals can perform" (Edelman 1985, 5-6). Thus, the political process becomes the arena in which we displace private emotions, especially strong anxieties and hopes. In this way, for most of the mass public, the political process is bound to become symbolic and emotional in impact, calling for conformity to promote social harmony and serving as the focus of psychological tensions. Especially when the people are suffering from war, revolutions, and deaths, there is a much greater need for reassuring symbols. Political symbols bring out in concentrated form those particular meanings and emotions that the members of a community create and reinforce in one another (Edelman 1985, 7-8).

Our brief examination of the symbolic dimension of politics will shed some meaningful light on Mr. Shin's selfless involvement in the joint memorial service and a series of revival services. In those meetings, Shin glorified the twelve martyrs and humiliated himself as the sinner who succumbed to torture and thereby betrayed God. That was, no doubt, a distortion of the factual truth he himself witnessed. Why did he voluntarily cooperate in manufacturing their martyrdom and enhancing the political cause while willingly humiliating himself before the public? How could he preach that God's truth and an afterlife in the eternal kingdom of God existed, while he himself seriously questioned God's existence and ceased to believe in said afterlife?

In order to understand this paradox, we need to briefly examine the meanings of war for the political community in general and of the June 25 War for Koreans in particular. Humankind has experienced two world wars in which millions of people had to die without knowing the reason for their deaths. The unprecedented scale of violence in the two world wars and the subsequent invention of nuclear weapons render war an utterly futile human enterprise, overshadowing the possibly positive functions it may have performed in the past, because the waging of war itself now runs the risk of wiping out all the members of the human community, not to mention the specific political community in whose name the war is waged.

Koreans had to participate in World War II under the Japanese banner and, soon after the liberation from Japanese colonial rule, had to undergo the June 25 War during the period of 1950-1953, the most devastating war in the history of Korea and one that claimed millions of lives. How meaningless and absurd the internecine civil war had been was vividly described in the novel, first through Captain Park's account of his hand-to-hand combat and second via Colonel Chang's sarcastic remark in response to Major Lee, who insisted that the truth about the twelve ministers be revealed:

> The trouble was that it was pitch-black night and that we all spoke Korean. Devil only knew which side we were killing. Everyone was shouting in the same language, "Who are you? Who are you?" . . . then something–panic, terror, you name it–snapped, and everyone was killing everyone else. (Kim 1964, 45-46)

> Or would you rather tell them this war is just like any other bloody war in the stinking history of idiotic mankind, that it is nothing but the result of a blind struggle for power among the beastly states, among the rotten politicians and so on, that thousands of people have died and more will die in this stupid war, for nothing, for absolutely nothing, because they are just innocent victims, helpless pawns in the arena of cold-blooded, calculating international power politics? (Kim 1964, 172-73)

As the war went on, Mr. Shin was constantly agonized by witnessing his poor, suffering people who were tortured by war, who were hungry, cold, sick, and weary of life. Therefore, he took one step further from his original position that he should never reveal his personal truth about faith–passive silence–and decided to actively lie to the people about the twelve murdered ministers, God's justice, and the afterlife in order to give them the hope needed to survive the horrible despair brought on by the war, even if this might turn out to be sheer illusion. In order to breathe hope into despairing souls, he had to give symbolic reassurance to those masses who were suddenly forced to face suffering and hardship in the name of the political community but were helpless in controlling their fate. Especially during war, when the very survival of the political community is at stake, the symbolic use of politics is urgently needed, because the political community is too strained to provide the same tangible benefits as in peacetime. The masses may remain apolitical as far as security is provided, but once war breaks out, they are fundamentally mobilized and uprooted, and politics once distant becomes omnipresent in their everyday life. All the values and morals that have hitherto held the community together are threatened from the root, as war is protracted without victory in clear sight.

Thus, by deliberately using the twelve martyrs as the sacrifice for their sins, a unifying symbol in a series of revival services, Shin wanted to renew the faith of Christians and rekindle the feelings of the community that was torn apart and warped by the devastating war. He usually began his sermons by saying, "I belong to you and you belong to me. I am you and you are me, and we are one. . . . We are here together as one to worship our God and praise him" (Kim 1964, 193). He stressed that they were all sinners, including himself, who had betrayed the twelve martyrs–a community of sufferings and sin–and told them to repent. Here the use of "we" represents the fact that Shin participated in the same sufferings of the masses and shared their fate.[7] The use of "we" is the beginning of politics, showing

7 As I shall discuss later, this might be the ultimate reason for Shin's refusal to

the recognition that we share in the same fate and we collectively take charge of our destiny to whatever extent is within our power. According to Hanna Pitkin, political discourse is not "a matter here, as in becoming a moral agent, of relating 'I' to 'you' or even 'I' to 'thou,' but of relating 'I' to 'we,' in a context where many other selves also have claims on that 'we'" (Pitkin 1981, 345).

In this sense, Shin's revival ceremonies and joint memorial service may turn out to be political rituals rehearsed in religious dress. Such rituals are motor activities that symbolically involve its participants in a common enterprise, calling their attention to their relatedness and mutual concern in a compelling way. It thereby both promotes unity and evokes satisfaction and solace in this unity. Humans instinctively seek meaning and order when placed in a confusing, ambiguous situation. This motor activity, performed together with others, reassures everyone that there are no dissenters and brings a sense of community in a collective enterprise. Signs and symbols–the martyred, in the novel–are the only means by which the masses not in a position to analyze a complex situation rationally, may adjust themselves to it and thereby reconcile with a stark reality. By using "we," Shin also maintained the appearance that he was not a manipulator of the symbols but their partaker. But in order to know whether this was really anything more than a rhetorical device, we need to examine the meaning of his death, the topic we now turn to.

retreat from Pyongyang with the South Korean troops.

Conclusion: The Meaning of Shin's Death

In an era of rampant mass propaganda and manipulation, those who speak to the people do not tell the truth, but only what they want their people to believe. Thus we trust no one and become cynical. Mr. Shin and Colonel Chang told the people what people wanted to believe and what they wanted people to believe, one for the sake of his religion and the other for his state. Can we condemn them for telling lies to their own people? If so, how do we deal with people who were susceptible to their lies? Are people blameless in their naïve attitude of succumbing to them? After all, it was not only Chang and Shin but also the very people who were responsible for the seemingly ridiculous but desperate play in which Lee felt cheated. When what the authorities want people to believe coincides with what people want to believe, we cannot place blame on one group only. When the victims of the deception willingly accept it, the deception becomes reciprocal in its nature, and what begins as a deception ends up becoming collective self-deception. The appearance of the community might be retained by this collective ritual, since "[i]n its political aspect, a community is held together not by truth but by consensus," which the members of a given community express by participating in the ritual (Wolin 2004, 58). Such participation reinforces the sense of belonging and protects the community from the forces of anomie.

Thus, there may be little difference among the joint memorial service, the election in contemporary democratic societies, and the rain dance or other seemingly irrational primitive rituals in the sense that all these collective activities partake of a symbolic dimension of our communal life. As Machiavelli uncannily notes, this symbolic dimension of politics will always be with us and occupy our political space, so long as there remains a gap between what ought to be done and what is actually done. So the twelve martyrs fill this gap and do at least tell us what we want to believe about ourselves, our religion, and our political community. But we have to take note of the cost our political community incurs as a result of this symbolic aspect of politics. When our political action becomes purely ritualistic, it may be dramatic in its form by entertaining spectators, and yet, at the same time, empty in substance. Politics will mainly supply symbols without meeting our tangible collective needs, through endless manipulation of abstract stereotypes, images, and words, and mass propaganda. This point is made poignantly by Lee when he says to Captain Park:

> You say you give them what they want? How do you know that a pack of lies is what they want? Are you sure that is what they need? They need truth. It may be painful, but truth is what they need and what you must give them. . . . I am tired, I am sick of all this pretension, all these noble lies, all in the name of people, for the people. And meanwhile the people continue to suffer, continue to die, deceived from birth to death. (Kim 1964, 212-13)

In other words, the symbolic dimension of politics serves to dull the critical faculties of the members of the community rather than arouse them. Lee makes this point when he says:

> You say you do all this for them, for their happiness. But no! You do it because you want your propaganda. You do it because you wanted to save your church from being scandalized. You do it because you wanted to deceive the people into believing that everything is going to be all right, that a god in heaven takes good care of them, that a state sincerely worries about their lot, and all this in the name of the people. (Kim 1964, 212-13).

From another perspective, we may examine Lee's position–that the truth should be revealed–more positively. As Hanna Pitkin points out, "What distinguishes politics . . . is action–the possibility of a shared, collective, deliberative, active intervention in our fate" (Pitkin 1981, 344). In order to render such action possible, we need a correct understanding of our reality, however painful it may be. Even the rulers in totalitarian and dictatorial regimes who mobilize each and every means possible to deceive their own people still need to collect information about reality in order to remain in power, to continue to deceive the people but escape self-deception. Therefore, it is only on the basis of true knowledge and information about what is true that we, or even the worst tyrant, can decide what is to be done. Lee seems to represent this attitude.

All this said, the final question remains to be answered. Were both Shin and Chang sincere in their motives when they "manufactured" the martyrdom? Did they not have some sinister motives of serving their own narrow religious or political interests? It would be almost impossible to penetrate into the innermost human psyche with definite certainty. However, their deaths are significant and suggestive. Even if they manufactured noble lies to keep the people from falling into a bottomless abyss of despair, they vindicated their cause, breathing life into their noble lies by their exemplary action and noble deaths, Chang as a soldier and Shin as a minister. When the situations demanded, they were willing to offer themselves for the political community and religious truth. Chang fulfilled his role as a member of the political community by dying for it–possibly the ultimate expression of the unity of the self and the political community. Shin refused to leave Pyongyang with the retreating South Korean troops and nobody knew about his last days. There were only conflicting rumors, and his martyrdom was never confirmed by a human witness. As Kenneth Burke points out, martyrdom is "vanity when addressed not to the Absolute Witness, but to human onlookers" (Burke 1969, 222). All in all, the actions of Chang and Shin seem to suggest the paradoxical yet enigmatic predicament of the contemporary world, in that "even if there is no truth, humans can be truthful, and even if there is no faith, humans can be faithful."[8]

8 Here I have made a modification of Arendt's remark: even if there is no truth, man can be truthful, and even if there is no reliable certainty, man can be reliable" (Arendt 1958, 279).

References

Arendt, Hannah. 1958. *The Human Condition.* Garden City, NY: Doubleday.

——. 1977. *Between Past and Future.* Harmondsworth: Penguin.

Burke, Kenneth. 1969. *A Rhetoric of Motives.* Berkeley: University of California Press.

Camus, Albert. 1947. *The Plague.* Translated by Stuart Gilbert. New York: Vintage Books.

——. 1954. *The Stranger.* Translated by Stuart Gilbert. New York: Vintage Books.

——. 1955. *The Myth of Sisyphus and Other Essays.* Translated by Justine O'Brien. New York: Vintage Books.

Edelman, Murray J. 1985. *The Symbolic Uses of Politics.* Champaign: University of Illinois Press.

Kim, Richard E. 1964. *The Martyred.* New York: George Braziller.

Machiavelli, Niccolò. 1981. *The Prince.* Translated by George Bull. Harmondsworth: Penguin.

Pitkin, Hanna F. 1972. *Wittgenstein and Justice.* Berkeley: University of California Press.

——. 1981. "Justice: On Relating Private and Public." *Political Theory* 9 (August): 327-51.

Schaar, John H. 1981. *Legitimacy in the Modern State.* New Brunswick, NJ: Transaction Books.

Weber, Max. 1958. "Politics as a Vocation." In *From Max Weber: Essays in Sociology,* translated and edited by H. H. Gerth and C. Wright Mills, 77-128. New York: Oxford University Press.

Wolin, Sheldon S. 2004. *Politics and Vision: Continuity and Innovation in Western Political Thought.* Expanded edition. Princeton, NJ: Princeton University Press.

INDEX

D

E

R

S

T